Bettering Humanity Through Communication & Cultures

Bettering Humanity Through Communication & Cultures

Editors

Maria Burguete & Jean-Patrick Connerade

Published by Science Matters Press
Cascais, Portugal
Quinta da Bicuda
R. das Perdizes, lote 11, n.º 154 - 1.ºA
2750-704 Torre
confsciencematters@gmail.com

ISBN: 1723301698
ISBN-13: 978-1723301698

The sixth Science Matters (Scimat) Conference "Bettering Humanity: Historic Secular Movements" was held at Cascais Cultural Centre, Cascais, Portugal in October 25-27, 2017.

Summary

Preface

This book arises from a very special conjunction between several different scientists meeting together for the **Xth anniversary of the Science Matters Conferences** at Cascais Cultural Center in October 2017.

For better resolution please download the poster in the following link:
Poster FINAL SCIMAT 2017 Julho.pdf (3848924).
Read more: https://www.scimat-2015.com/

A special place with special people on a special occasion to celebrate the X th birthday of the new multidiscipline called *Science Matters.*

Appropriately, in February 2018 the very first Science Matters Center emerged in Cascais, the European Youth Capital for 2018 (see European **Youth Capital 2018: Cascais** European Youth Forum).

Its three founding members are:

Maria Burguete, Raul Sardinha and João Miguel Pais.

Later on, in May 2018, the non-profit Association was established with its eleven members, through which we can witness real interdisciplinarity in action – **The Scimat Association:**

1. MARIA BURGUETE – Chemical Engineer/Biochemistry/History and Philosophy of Science.
2. RAUL SARDINHA – Agronomy Engineer and Manager of Higher Education Institutions.
3. JOÃO MIGUEL PAIS – Fine Arts & Sculpture.
4. DULCE PAIS – Applied Mathematics.
5. JEAN-PATRICK CONNERADE – Physics and Poetry (President of European Academy of Sciences, Arts and Literature).
6. MÁRIO MATOS SILVA – Economy & Financial Manager.
7. ANABELA DELGADO – Agronomy Engineer.
8. FLORENTIN BOSSE – Financial Sciences.
9. MANUEL BICHO – Medical Sciences.
10. MARIA CLARA BICHO – Medical Sciences.
11. LEONOR BELTRÀN – Performance & Plastic Arts.

Now, let us return to the book contents: **chapter 1** written by Claudine Cohen with ***Jean Jacques Rousseau (1712-1778) on bettering humanity: Music, Education and Politics.*** Rousseau belongs to the group of French-speaking philosophers including also Voltaire, Diderot, D'Alembert and others, who created the

Enlightenment movement and were indirectly the instigators of the French Revolution. Rousseau was probably the most 'revolutionary' of the group and so his influence on the birth of modern European society was considerable.

Chapter 2 written by Jean-Patrick Connerade concerns ***The Contribution of British Atheist Reformers in the nineteenth Century.*** This article puts into context the activities of the British atheists who became prominent European writers and thinkers during and after the French Revolution. Most prominent amongst them was Jeremy Bentham, sometimes referred to as 'the English Voltaire' who saw himself as a social reformer and whose hobby was drafting new constitutions for new nations, compatible with the 'Spirit of the Times'. He was active in promoting the cause of Greek Independence, in which he managed to involve Lord Byron, and many of his most advanced ideas of social reform are actually implemented by contemporary society. Indeed, they have become accepted in our daily lives in many parts of the world.

Chapter 3 presents ***The Vienna Circle and the role of Positivism*** by Annette Vogt. The Vienna Circle had a profound influence on philosophy and on the birth of positivism in Europe, extending out to the United Kingdom, where positivism was very influential. The principles which were elaborated in that time were influenced by the development of modern science (in particular: Relativity and Quantum Mechanics) and, conversely, many scientists of the time were influenced by the new philosophical concepts originating from the Vienna School in their description of reality.

Chapter 4 deals with interdisciplinary theory by Florentin Bosse through his paper ***Letters Matters, Mathematics and Bibliotherapy.*** How living with science and living with Letters and with the Arts are interconnected in the modern world is a fundamental question for citizens in our own times. It is inescapable that we all have to discover these interconnections within ourselves in order to develop personalities in tune with the new century, but little has been done to facilitate the task because of the inherited dominance of specialization. Florentin Bosse explores the area of adaptation of the human psyche to the multi-disciplinary world of today, which has become all-important in contemporary thought.

In **Chapter 5** Manuel Mota allow us to see how Biology is still a principal activity within the history of humanity in his ***Bettering Humanity through Biology.***

Chapter 6 written by Nigel Sanitt provides an answer to the question: How is meaning created in science and what part do questions play in scientific theories? through his very interesting paper ***The Eye in Ideas: Culture, Curiosity and Communication in Scientific Discovery.***

Chapter 7 exemplifies how Arts can better humanity and the whole involved process is presented by João Miguel Pais & Maria Burguete in ***A Truly Knowledgeable Person must first be an Attentive Questioner.***

Finally the **Chapter 8** presents an artist self-portrait since her very beginning as a dancer, a painter and a teacher of Arts ***A Look at the (my) Creative Process*** by Leonor Beltràn.

MARIA BURGUETE
Rocha Cabral Institute, Lisbon, Portugal

JEAN-PATRICK CONNERADE
European Academy of Sciences, Arts and Letters, Paris, France

Abstracts of the Lectures

Jean-Jacques Rousseau on Bettering Humanity: Music, Politics and Education

CLAUDINE COHEN
Professor (Directeur d'Etudes) at the Ecole des Hautes Etudes en sciences Sociales (Centre de Recherche sur les Arts et le Langage). (claudine.cohen@ehess.fr)

"There is (...) a specific quality which distinguishes Humans from the animals, and which cannot be disputed: it is the ability to perfect oneself," writes Jean-Jacques Rousseau in his *Discourse on the origin of inequality among Men* (1755). Perfectibility, a "distinctive faculty," which is "almost unlimited," is the condition for an improvement of humanity, which in his eyes should be carried out first on the political and social level. In his successive works, *Le Contrat social* (1762), *l'Emile* (1762), and his posthumous *Essai sur l'origine des langues,* he lays the principles for such improvements.

If Rousseau describes human history as an irreversible degradation from a good nature, he also believes there are ways, in turn, of bettering this condition, which should be first sought on the political level. Through the "Social Contract" humans take hold of their own destiny: a democratic social state, chosen "by substituting justice to instinct, and giving one's actions the moral dimension they did not have before", can provide collective strength and freedom that the individual loses when in a group governed by "the law of the strongest".

Moreover, a revolution in education is a prerequisite for any revolution in ethics and society. Unlike empiricists whose educational principles aim to imprint knowledge as on a "soft wax," Rousseau considers it necessary to recognize the specific nature a child's mind and to follow the natural development of a child's instincts. Educators must train children by drawing their own strength toward progress to find their place in the social world. Sensitive, intuitive and active methods should be preferred to teaching with words. Language, born of emotion, of passion, of desire, was originally the expression of human sensitivity, before it became loaded with rational value. Music tries to reconnect with the roots of the human language and psyche, and exalts all the richness of this sensitivity.

Rousseau based his views on bettering humanity on the principle of humans' own perfectibility and freedom. His concepts of human improvement at the social and personal levels are deeply rooted in a political and ethical vision, contrasting with attempts to impose, "from the outside", authoritarian criteria for bettering humanity of which recent history provides dismal examples. The principles he outlines may be valuable for thinking critically for instance, in today's world, "transhumanist" ambitions to enhance human intellect and physiology through technological devices.

CLAUDINE COHEN is a philosopher and science historian. She is a Professor at the Ecole des Hautes Etudes en Sciences Sociales (Paris), and a Cumulative Professor at the Earth and Life Science section of the Ecole Pratique des Hautes Etudes. Her research and publications deal, notably, with the history of early modern Life and Earth Sciences. Among her works : the first English edition of Leibniz's *Protogaea*, The

University of Chicago Press, 2008 (with André Wakefield), *Sciences, libertinage et clandestinité à l'aube des Lumières: le Transformisme de telliamed,* Paris Presses Universitaires de France 2011, and *La Méthode de Zadig, La Trace, le fossile, la preuve,* Paris, Editions du Seuil, 2011.

The Contribution of British Atheist Reformers in the XIXth Century

JEAN-PATRICK CONNERADE
Quantum Optics and Laser Science Group, Physics Department, Imperial College London SW72BW and European Academy of Sciences Arts and Letters 60 rue Monsieur le Prince 75006 Paris (jean-patrick@connerade.com).

British atheist thinkers have played a very important intellectual and reformist part. However, with the sole exception of Darwin, they are mostly ignored, despite a profound influence on European development and on Western Art during the nineteenth century.

The paradox of an industrially progressive nation with a reactionary social structure was precisely the opposite of the mainstream situation in Europe, where industry generally lagged behind the times and rapid social change induced political instability. The Romantic Movement in the UK split into two very different strands. On the one hand were the rabid revolutionaries. On the other were the 'bourgeois Romantics', mainly of the Manchester school. The conflict between the two was ideologically profound. The Manchester poets were pretty conventional in their principles and seldom expressed religious views. Even the opium eaters amongst them found a comfortable place as established artists in a well-regulated society. In contrast, such characters as Byron,

Shelley and their friends were far more radical in outlook and some carried their opinions and lifestyle to the point of provocation.

When Shelley fled Britain with not just one but both of Godwin's daughters, his behavior was considered so dreadful that he became an exile on the Continent. Lord Byron was in the same position, having had a daughter by his own sister and being consequently ostracized by high society. In Switzerland, they developed the gothic novel, and that Mary Shelley began to put together her *Frankenstein,* which was to become the emblematic anti-science book.

Although the poet Shelley had ambitions as a social reformer, the true innovator in this field was Jeremy Bentham. He is often referred to as 'the English Voltaire' but is reality was quite different. He was a co-founder of University College London which, because of his influence and that of his circle, became the first institution of higher education with no religious affiliation whatsoever and thus open to non-believers. Amongst the most important reforms introduced by Bentham during his lifetime was the idea of opening the doors of the University to female students, which happened at University College for the first time in Europe. Initially, they were only allowed in as free auditors but not registered as full-time students. Soon, however, Bentham insisted that they should be allowed to sit examinations and obtain qualifications, which was an amazing and controversial step. This, without doubt, is the pioneering spirit which attracted many brilliant female writers to reside in the same district of London, giving rise to what later became known as *the Bloomsbury set.* Bentham founded the *Committee for Greek Independence,* which met on several occasions at the Anchor pub in London. He convinced Lord Byron to join. The manifesto they all signed, calling for Greek independence, was published in the Morning Chronicle. Byron equipped the military ship the Hercules which took him to Greece and to his death at Missolonghi.

JEAN-PATRICK CONNERADE is Emeritus Professor at Imperial College London & the East China University of Shanghai, Permanent Guest Researcher, Wuhan Institute of Physics and Mathematics & President of the European Academy of Sciences Arts and Letters under the aegis of UNESCO.

The Vienna Circle and the role of Positivism

ANNETTE B. VOGT
Max Planck Institute for the History of Science, Boltzmannstr. 22, 14195 Berlin, FR Germany (vogt@mpiwg-berlin.mpg.de)

The history of positivism as a philosophical theory goes back to the 18th century when the French philosopher Auguste Comte (1798--1857) had published his volume. Among the most important thinker to develop the concept of positivism are the French philosopher Emil Durkheim (1858-1917) and the Austrian scholar Ernst Mach (1838--1916). In the early 20th century the capital Vienna became a center for discussions on positivism as well as for the further developments, also known as neo-positivism – the "Vienna Circle" became a synonym for this development, where philosophers and mathematicians, economists and sociologists were discussing together and against each other. Because of the Nazi's, first in 1933 in Germany, from 1938 on in Austria, most of these important scientists, philosophers and scholars who were representatives of the Vienna Circle and/or involvend in the develoment of the "unified science" had to go into exile. Thus, the USA became the new home country of this philosophical discipline.

First, I sketch out the definitions of positivism, as a philosophical theory, compared with empiricism, in conflict with metaphysics and theology, and the later developments, known as logical positivism, neo-positivism, and post-positivism.

Second, I'll describe the history of the famous "Vienna Circle", the three periods from 1907 to 1912, from 1918 to 1924, and from 1924 to 1936/38. In 1929 "The Manifesto" of the Vienna Circle was declared, an initiative of Otto Neurath (1882-1945), an economist and sociologist, and the ideal of the "unified science" was announced. In the 1920s a small group was also working in Berlin, at the Berlin University around Hans Reichenbach (1891-1953). From 1920 until 1933 at the same Philosophical Faculty the mathematician and aerodynamicist Richard von Mises (1883-1953) was teaching, the other great representative of the theory of probability together with Ladislaus von Bortkiewicz (1868-1932), and an outspoken positivist, influenced by the Vienna Circle. Later in exile R. von Mises published his book "Positivism. A Study in human understanding" (1939, 1951). A friend of R. von Mises (and of Albert Einstein too) was the physicist and mathematician Philipp Frank (1884-1964) who was professor at the Prague University from 1912 to 1938 and called a "Machist".

Third, in my talk, I'll describe the fate, the circumstances, and the content and aims of the publication of Richard von Mises' book "Positivism. A Study in human understanding". Published as Volume I of a planned series "Library of unified science, book series" it came out in German (Kleines Lehrbuch des Positivismus) in a publishing house in The Hague in 1939, shortly before the beginning of WW II. This book had a special fate, as the series with the editors Otto Neurath, Rudolf Carnap, Philipp Frank, Jorgen Jorgensen, and Charles W. Morris. An english translation of this book was published in 1951, and only in 1990 it was re-published in German.

ANNETTE B. VOGT obtained her diploma in mathematics and her PhD in history of mathematics, both from the University of Leipzig.

Prof. Vogt is a research scholar at the Max Planck Institute for the History of Science in Berlin. She published several books and more than 150 scientific papers. Since 2013 she is serving as assistant secretary general of the Council of the DHST/IUHPST; from 2005 to 2013 she was President of the Women's Commission in the DHST.

Letters Matters, Bibliotherapy and Musical Mathematics

FLORENTIN BOSSE
Investment Banking Risk Analyst (Bank of New York, Deutsche Bank, Lloyds Bank), entrepreneur (founder of Swapstream and innovator – Patent US20090265264) and bibliotherapist (Letters Matters) (florentin.bosse@gmail.com)

The interdisciplinary theory(*) is the very proof that the categorisation thinking, the alleged "inner desire" to put things that we see or think into boxes has a limited value and it emphasises in the meantime the fluidity of space, time and reality (which are questionable entities in themselves)…The glue that brings the different elements of our rationale called "disciplines", as well as humanities, social sciences and science together is intensity of the each of our undertakings and its variations of intensity. Literature, bibliotherapy and mathematics converge in enriching one's life. By considering possible definitions of what a novel or a mathematical structure is, it is argued that the fundamental difference between conventional mathematics and artistic literature is one of form rather than content and bibliotherapy – one could say that self-bibliotherapy – is the magic wand that shapes both

---

(*) Rick Szostak – Defining interdisciplinarity
https://sites.google.com/a/ualberta.ca/rick-szostak/research/about-interdisciplinarity/
definitions/defining-instrumental-interdisciplinarity

mathematics and artistic literature in a subliminal, intense journey. But apart from arguing the above, the very living proof of applied interdisciplinary theory is in front of your eyes.

It all started October 2015, when I returned from my six months self-exile from society – or, "retreat", the word people use nowadays for the time one needs to question the unquestionable questions – undertaking a solitary pilgrimage from Berlin to Santiago de Compostella and then further to Portugal; a pilgrimage which brought me back trust, nature, wisdom and love. I started that pilgrimage after working 30 years in technology, using mathematics, logical thinking and questioning, rationale and abstraction. I came back from that pilgrimage with a clear sense of purpose and a mission.

Perhaps all started a long time ago, when I was Robinson Crusoe, D'Artagnan, Holden Caulfield, Oliver Twist, Prince Myshkin, and many others…while exceling in math, physics and chemistry at school, as science matters were by large as the best socially accepted recipe for a successful, reliable and rewarding professional life.

FLORENTIN BOSSE was born in Bucharest, Romania, made academic studies and graduated with a Master in Computer Science in 1980. Emigrated to United States and continued working in the computer industry and in parallel got a Master in Computer Databases at NYU. He started his career in Investment Banking at the Bank of New York in 1985. He relocated to Germany in 1987 where he continued his career in Investment Banking, in different Banks (Citibank, Deutsche Bank, Lloyds Bank, Commerzbank, HypoVereinsbank, Chicago Mercantile Exchange) in different places (London, Paris, Frankfurt, München, Prague, Chicago). In the year 2000 he started his own company – Swapstream – and left the Banking industry, building and operating an independent electronic platform for trading derivatives and getting a registered patent in Chicago for the computer modelling of the financial mathematics involved in trading. He retired in 2014 and became bibliotherapist in his book lovers' shop "Letters Matters" in Lisbon.

Bettering Humanity through Biology

MANUEL GALVÃO DE MELO E MOTA
Centro de Estudos de História e Filosofia da Ciência/Instituto de História Contemporânea, (CEHFiC/IHC) and Department of Biology, University of Évora, 7002-554 Évora, Portugal (mmota@uevora.pt)

B iology is arguably referred to as the "science of the XXIth century". This prestigious title intrinsically contains a huge responsibility. For many centuries, Biology has contributed directly or indirectly to bettering humankind, although obvious and objective effects have only became evident since the XIXth century. There are three main domains to which Biology has made significant contributions: Agriculture, Environment and Medicine. Several scientific disciplines connected to Biology have been involved such as Genetics (mendelian and molecular), Cell Biology, Ecology, Microbiology, and what was known for a long time as "Natural History" (today we would include these roughly within Botany and Zoology). Agronomy, a relatively recent science, has made a tremendous impact by providing knowledge on growing plants and animals, and developing new and better crops. One specific moment in time, following World War II, known as the "Green Revolution" benefitted humanity immensely, by combating hunger in countries such as India and Mexico. The "father" of the Green Revolution, Norman Borlaug, was awarded the 1970 Peace Nobel Prize for such achievement. In the XXIth century, biologists and agronomists are working hard to develop new and better crops to feed almost

8 billion people. In the medical field, the contributions are innumerable, from the discovery and development of vaccines (Jenner and Pasteur), to antibiotics (Fleming) and combatting diseases. This has increased the average life expectancy of humans from around 30-40 in the beginning of the XXth century, to a present value of around 75 (depending on the country). These achievements have been recognized by society, through dozens of Nobel Prizes in Medicine. All these successes have been made possible through Biology. In the past 30-40 years, numerous voices have been raised alerting for the environmental degradation of our planet, its land and oceans, its biomes and ecosystems. We have been depleting our planet at an incredible rate. But today, biologists and environmental scientists have the knowledge and tools to better the planet. We know how the ecosystems function and what causes harm them. There is still time, together with a strong public opinion, to halt the damage. Once again, Biology is a principal actor.

MANUEL MOTA is a biologist (Univ. Lisbon, 1982), completed a PhD *(as a Fulbright scholar)* in Virginia Tech (USA) in 1992, in Plant Pathology (Phytonematology), and has since worked mainly with plant parasitic nematodes, with a strong emphasis on the recent biological invasion known as "pine wilt disease". He has published over 100 papers and book chapters in major international journals such as *Molecular Plant Pathology, Trends in Parasitology, PLoS, Planta, Forest Pathology, Nematology, New Phytologist, Mol. Phylogenetics and Evolution, Ann. Appl. Biology,* etc. He is editor of 2 books (in Brill and Springer, two major scientific publishers). His is a regular referee for 20 major scientific journals. He teaches several courses of Biology at the University of Évora (UE), and ULHT (Lisbon), and has taught at other universities (Kyoto, Prague, Nottingham, Va. Tech, UENF/Darcy Ribeiro and UFV (Viçosa, MG), Brasil, etc.). His scientific activity has attracted significant funding (over € 1 million) to the UE, mainly through national and international research projects. Besides strict biological courses, he also maintains interest in History and Epistemology of Biology, and has taught Bioethics and History of Biology.

The Eye in Ideas: Culture, Curiosity and Communication in Scientific Discovery.

NIGEL SANITT
Pantaneto Press, 3 Gordon Street, Luton, Bedfordshire, LU1 2QP, UK.
(Nigel@pantaneto.co.uk)

How is meaning created in science and what part do questions play in scientific theories?

Many aspects of research activity in science are opaque to outsiders and this opacity infects how connections are made between science and other disciplines. We have this tremendous feeling that science has progressed, which has resulted in technological advancement beyond anything we have seen before.

The only blemish on this scenario is that the foundations of science seem to be built on sand. Theories come and go and truth is elusive to understanding, even a hindrance. Knowledge acquisition appears to be an end in itself, as though knowledge is some sort of commodity or object that can be traded. We have created a mythical objective world, where we pretend that opinions and values are generated by data alone and not by people, or worse scientists.

Scientists bask in the new technological Atlantis, oblivious to the mismatch between quantum mechanics and general relativity – our two most important physical theories, and revelling in the fact that the nature of most of the matter in the universe is anybody's guess.

Science is part of our culture and part of the understanding of science now, and in the past, is bound up with recognising the social, economic and political ramifications as they apply to science.

In this talk I put forward a radical interpretation of how science works to address these questions and try to put science in its rightful context of a means of helping us to engage with our world.

Nigel Sanitt gained his Ph.D. at the Institute of Astronomy, Cambridge University, where he helped lay the foundations of gravitational lensing research. He is editor of an online journal *The Pantaneto Forum,* which is devoted to science communication and founder and chief executive of the *Pantaneto Press,* which publishes books in the physical sciences. He has published a number of articles, one book as editor and one book as author – Routledge Revivals: Science as a Questioning Process (1996), He has also published two novels under the pen name Norman Stanton.

A Truly Knowledgeable Person must first be an Attentive Questioner

João Miguel Pais
Department of Painting, University of Lisbon, Faculty of Fine Arts, Portugal – (jmpais55@gmail.com)
Maria Burguete
Scientist at Bento da Rocha Cabral Institute, Lisboa, Portugal
(scimat2018@gmail.com)

Western civilization grew out of two cultural branches – the Judeo-Christian and the Latin – which, if we really consider them deeply, are not that different in terms of their "hidden" roots. Is it possible to scientifically validate much of the way in which these traditions have empirically supposed the world can be understood? If so, how? Mere metaphors!?...

Today, we must to some extent be capable of asking whether there is any truth in these philosophical concepts.

We believe that both the so-called exact sciences and the human sciences are able to help us organize and order our thoughts. We know that thought doesn't arise *a priori,* but results from an act and from curiosity about natural phenomena – a curiosity that drives us to find a way to explain them. A combination of mere theoretical speculation from the past and established scientific knowledge can reveal a culture that is sensitive and creative, or even "intuitive" if it comes close to some of the concepts accepted by today's science.

An unprejudiced reading of authors as different as Plato and António Damásio, among others, allows us to discover theses that help us understand that which unites us and distinguishes us as humanity. On one thing, we can all agree – we have always been very curious and very creative.

If we take these assumptions as our starting point, our abstract begins to make sense. What we want to show is that there really is an interaction between the areas of knowledge of the human and the exact sciences. In particular, we ask how to characterize the specificity of the former in relation to the latter and vice versa; and at what point do these forms of knowledge meet?... These are the questions to which we will seek rigorous, documented answers.

JOÃO MIGUEL PAIS obtained his Ph.D. with The Light in Painting Representation: Myth Representation and Light in the Pictoric Practice (1550-1650), from University of Lisbon, Faculty of Fine Arts, in 2014.

MARIA BURGUETE received her Ph.D in History of Science from Ludwig Maximilians University at Munich, Germany (2000). She graduated from the Faculty of Sciences in Lisbon (1982), after completing a Bachelor Degree in Chemical Engineering (1979). A scientist and University Lecturer with large teaching & research experience in a wide variety of fields. Author of scientific books, and experience as conference organizer of International Scientific Meetings since 2006. This diversity enhanced the development of both her interdisciplinarity and transdisciplinarity. She is a scientist at Bento da Rocha Cabral in Portugal since 2007. She has published nine scientific books and seven poetry books, and over 25 scientific papers mostly in history and philosophy of science. Since 2010 she is a fellow of the European Academy of Sciences, Arts & Letters, founded in Paris in 1980. Recently, she created the First **Science Matters Center (Associação Scimat-Portugal/A Non-Profit Cultural Association).**

A look at the (my) creative process

LEONOR BELTRÁN
(leonor.beltran@netcabo.pt)

Jean Jacques Rousseau (1712-1778) on bettering humanity: Music, Education and Politics

Claudine Cohen

"A great deal of art is needed to prevent social man from being entirely artificial."

(Rousseau, *Emile*, Book IV)

If Rousseau describes human history as an irreversible degradation from a good nature, he also believes there are ways, in turn, of bettering this condition, which should be first sought on the political level. Through the «Social Contract» humans take hold of their own destiny: a democratic social state, chosen «by substituting justice to instinct, and giving one's actions the moral dimension they did not have before", can provide collective strength and freedom that the individual loses when in a group governed by "the law of the strongest".

Moreover, a revolution in education is a prerequisite for any revolution in ethics and society. Unlike empiricists whose educational principles aim to imprint knowledge as on a «soft wax,» Rousseau considers it necessary to recognize the specific nature of a child's mind and to follow the natural development of a child's instincts. Educators must train children by drawing their own strength toward progress to find their place in the social world. Sensitive, intuitive and active methods should be preferred to teaching with words. Language, born of emotion, of passion, of desire, was originally the expression of human sensitivity, before it became loaded with rational value. Music tries to reconnect with the roots of the human language and psyche, and exalts all the richness of this sensitivity.

Rousseau based his views on bettering humanity on the principle of humans' own perfectibility and freedom. His concepts of human improvement at the social and personal levels are deeply rooted in a political and ethical vision, contrasting with attempts to impose, «from the outside», authoritarian criteria for bettering humanity, of which recent history provides dismal examples. The principles he outlines may be valuable for thinking critically for instance, in today's world, «transhumanist» ambitions to enhance human intellect and physiology through technological devices.

Jean-Jacques Rousseau (1712-1778) is one of the best known and most influential philosophers of the French Enlightenment, whose thinking is credited to have had a strong influence on the 1789 French Revolution[1]. He wrote several important philosophical and political essays, among which le *Discours sur l'origine de l'inégalité parmi les hommes* (1755), *Le Contrat Social* (1862), and a major treatise on education, *L'Emile* (1762). In addition he authored a famous and well received novel, *La Nouvelle Héloïse* (1761), in which he recalled and applied, through fiction, his philosophical views, and Les *Confessions*, which was posthumously published in 1782-89, and is recognized as the foundation of the literary genre of autobiography in France.

Rousseau was born in Geneva on June 28, 1712 to a modest family. His mother, Suzanne Bernard, died a week after he was born. His brother soon ran away from home and his father, Isaac Rousseau, left Geneva to avoid imprisonment. Jean-Jacques was raised by an uncle and sent to study in the village of Bosey as an apprenticed to an engraver. In 1725 he went to Annecy to escape a violent master, and met there in 1728 Madame de Warens, receiving from her intellectual, spiritual, artistic and sentimental education

---

[1] See Mona Ozouf, *L'Homme régénéré, Essais sur le Révolution française,* Paris, Gallimard, 2013; François Furet, *Penser la Révolution française,* Paris, Gallimard Folio, 2013.

while he lived with her at les Charmettes between 1735 et 1737. In 1742, he finally left to Paris where he met with the Philosophers of the French capital, and started building up and publishing his own philosophical and political thinking. Throughout his life, Rousseau also extensively wrote on botany, on music and language and composed musical works. He wrote a two volumes *Dictionary of Music*[2] and a *Treatise on the origin of languages*, which remained unfinished, and was published posthumously.

One central issue in Rousseau's thinking is human perfectibility[3], at the individual as well as collective levels. "There is (...) a specific quality which distinguishes man from animal, and on which there can be no dispute, it is the ability to perfect oneself,» writes Rousseau in his *Discourse on the origin of inequality*. Perfectibility, a «distinctive faculty,» which is «almost unlimited,» is the very condition for human improvement, which in his eyes should be carried out first on the political and social levels. At the individual level, education is a key to personal improvement, and aims, in Rousseau's term, toward transforming the child into an adult who is in accordance with his own nature and with his real needs.On the level of interchange between individuals, language, born of emotion, of passion, and desire, is the original expression of human sensitivity, only later did it become loaded with rational meaning. Music tries to reconnect with the roots of the human language and psyche, and exalts all the richness of its original expressivity.

Here we will analyze Rousseau's vision on "bettering humanity" focusing on these three different modes of action: politics, education and music.

---

[2] Rousseau, *Dictionnaire de musique*, 1768.

[3] Henri Gouhier, «la "perfectibilité" selon J.-J. Rousseau», *Revue de Théologie et de Philosophie*. Troisième série, Vol. 110, No. 4 (1978), pp. 321-339.

I – Politics: improving the human condition

In his *Discours sur l'Origine de l'Inégalité parmi les hommes*[4] (1755) Rousseau describes human history as a degradation from a good and free nature, to a quasi state of slavery: "Man was born free, and everywhere he is in chains". Inequality comes from property, which bequeathes the "law of the strongest".

"The first man who, having encircled a field, thought to say: "This is mine", and found people simple enough to believe it, was the true founder of civil society. How many crimes, wars, murders, miseries and horrors would have spared a man who, tearing out the stakes or filling the ditch, would have shouted to his fellows: "Beware of listening to this impostor; you are lost, if you forget that the fruits belong to all, and that the earth belongs to no one".

But there is great appearance, that then things had already come to the point of no longer being able to last as they were; because this idea of property, depending on many previous ideas which could only be born successively, did not suddenly form in the human spirit. It was necessary to make progress, acquire industry and lights, transmit them and increase them from age to age, before arriving at the latter term of the state of nature", Rousseau wrote in the first pages of his *Discours sur l'Origine de l'Inégalité*.

If Rousseau described human history as an irreversible degradation, he also believed that ways of improving this condition exist[5],

---

[4] Jean-Jacques Rousseau, *A Discourse Upon the Origin and the Foundation of the Inequality Among Mankind;* translated by Donald A. Cress; introduced by James Miller, Hackett Press, Indianapolis, 1992. See also Peter Gay, *The Basic Political Writings of Jean-Jacques Rousseau,* Hackett Press, Indianapolis, 1987.

[5] On this process, namely on the concept of "supplement" in Rousseau's thought, see Jacques Derrida, *Of Grammatology*, John's Hopkins University Press, 1974.

namely on the political level. Through the «Social Contract»[6] men take control over their own destiny: a democratic social state, freely chosen «by substituting justice to instinct, and giving one's actions the moral dimension they did not have before", can provide men collectively with strength and freedom which the individual loses in a community governed by "the law of the strongest". Rousseau's "social contract" is the agreement through which each person enters into civil society. The contract binds people into a community that exists for mutual preservation. Thus under the social contract, everyone will be free because everyone will give up the same amount of freedom and receive the same amount of responsibility. In fact, through the social contract, people sacrifice their physical freedom to gain civil freedom.

Rousseau believed peoples could govern themselves: he saw freedom not as the liberty of doing whatever one wants but as the opportunity to do the right thing: this included obedience to authority, an authority agreed on by the citizens. "The legislative power belongs to the people, and can belong to it alone." (…) "Every law the people have not ratified in person is null and void – is, in fact, not a law."

Rousseau thus demonstrates that there is no right but instituted. Freedom, security and property are not natural human rights, they are instituted rights of the citizen. Similarly, political authority cannot be based on a natural and hereditary right, but on the general will of the people. "The Sovereign, having no force other than the legislative power, acts only by means of the laws; and the laws being solely the authentic acts of the general will, the Sovereign cannot act save when the people is assembled." The negation of the idea of natural right does not lead Rousseau to relativism, but to propose a model of

---

[6] Rousseau, *The Social Contract and later political writings*, ed. by Viktor Gourevitch, Cambridge University Press, 1997.

political constitution – a unique and secure rule of constitution: the Republic, which consists in the submission of each individual to the general will, in order to preserve everyone's freedom.

Rousseau did not invent the notion of a social contract[7]. Before him, Grotius, Hobbes and Locke had elaborated their own visions starting with a similar topic. However, Rousseau's contract, contrary to Hobbes', is *essentially democratic:* the citizens themselves – and not a monarch – are in charge of protecting their own lives and freedom. Each people elaborates its own rules and organization. Rousseau's views suppose *direct democracy* (and not representative democracy). This is why his political principles can best be applied to smaller states, like the Republic of Geneva.

II – Bettering humanity on individual grounds Rousseau's principles of education

A revolution in education is a prerequisite for any revolution in ethics and society. "Make the citizen good by training, and everything else will follow", Rousseau wrote. According to him, Humans are good by nature[8] – it is society's institutions that corrupt them. Children are naturally good and innocent.

"We do not know what childhood is" writes Rousseau in the introduction of *Emile*, in which he urges educators to take the child for what he is. «Children have ways of thinking and feeling of their own. It is absurd to want to substitute ours. Nature has made children

---

[7] See R. Derathé, *Jean-Jacques Rousseau et la science politique de son temps*, Paris, Vrin, 1950; Christopher W. Morris (ed.) *The Social Contract Theorists Critical Essays on Hobbes, Locke, and Rousseau.* Rowman & Littlefield Publishers, 1998.

[8] Arthur M. Melzer The Natural Goodness of Man: On the System of Rousseau's Thought, The University of Chicago Press, 1990.

to be loved and helped. "Unlike empiricists whose educational principles aim to impress knowledge upon the child's mind as on a «soft wax», Rousseau considers it necessary to recognize the nature the child's mind and to follow the natural development of children's instincts. Rousseau encourages educators to follow the natural evolution of a child through its successive stages, to address his senses and favor direct observation through the discovery of the natural world, to cultivate experiments and active methods.

Written between 1757 and 1760, *Emile or On Education* was published in the Spring of 1762. This bulky work of several hundred pages is divided into five books – each one corresponding to a phase of physical and moral development from birth to marriage. Emile – a rich and noble orphan raised from childhood by a governor – is a purely imaginary character, a staging of the author to expose his educational project. The complete cycle of Emile's education comprises four periods. The first five years should promote the physical development of the child and strengthen the body without constraint. Contact with the world occurs through the senses and according to nature. During the second period (5 to 12 years of age), Emile plays, exercises and strengthens his body, his organs, his senses, and his character in contact with natural realities, in a well-regulated freedom, without active intervention of his preceptor, who should not anticipate the natural evolution, and know how to waste time. «Dare I expose here the largest, the most important, the most useful rule of education? It's not about saving time, it's about losing it"[9]. «Children's education is a profession in which you need to know how to waste time to succeed"[10], Rousseau wrote.

---

[9] *Emile, or On Education,* book II.
[10] Ibid.

The preceptor takes part more directly in Emile's education during the third period of 12 to 15 years of age. By exploring the natural world, through travels, experience and observation of nature, Emile learns physics, chemistry, astronomy, geography, utilitarian and practical knowledge. To prepare for social life, he learns a manual job: Emile will be a carpenter. The fourth period is the age of passions. From 15 to 20 years of age, Emile then receives a moral and religious education. He discover philosophers, and God in nature without idolatry. His mentor channels his natural passions and his awakening to desire based on positive values such as pity, sympathy, friendship, charity. Worthy and modest, Emile is ready to enter the world.

The educational principles exposed in *Emile* appeared as quite innovative, compared with those in use in France under Louis the XVth's reign. While he elaborated them, Rousseau was probably inspired by a reflection on his own childhood. Without a mother from birth and very early left to himself, he was indiscriminately put into contact with books, whose dangerous influence impressed upon him the predominance of passions over concepts. «I had no idea of things, but all feelings were already known to me. I had not designed anything I had felt". Rousseau urges his contemporaries to allow children to mature rather than set them too early to conform to adult society. According to him, free negative education must preserve the natural qualities of the child, respect the spontaneous development of his personality. Unlike conventional educators who want to make him a good Christian, a good citizen, a good soldier, a good worker, etc. Rousseau breaks the molds by saying that the child must not become anything other than a fair human being. «Life is the job I want to teach him. When I leave my hands, he will not be a magistrate, a soldier, or a priest: he will be a man above all.»

Rousseau refuses to feed children with pre-digested texts and pre-established judgments that lock up their minds more than they educate them. He is against learning by heart texts whose meaning children do not master. Rousseau puts the child at the heart of the education process, which today is still an extremely modern concept.

The book was widely read, and thus shaped a new image of childhood and disrupted educational habits. Rousseau's treatise on education was a success without precedent in enlightened circles[11]. This success probably responded to an evolution of the family starting in the 1750s. According to Elisabeth Badinter, *Emile* is «the starting point of the modern family based on maternal love»[12]. This new image of childhood is also present in the works of by painters[13], such as Greuze, who now enhanced the representations of everyday life, raised at the level of history painting. Portraits of children or family portraits around the child became a major theme in painting[14]. These were the mark of the discovery of childhood and the attention that society now gave to its children. Rousseau's *Emile*, a pedagogical revolutionary, goes along with a change in the status of the child, even if the new model spread only very slowly.

Until nowadays, *Emile* remains one of the best read books about the education of children, because it raises essential questions. From the 18th century to the present, a number of innovative practitioner educators were inspired by *Emile*. However, Rousseau's ideas on education also raised controversies in his time, as well as in ours.

---

[11] Gilbert Py, *Rousseau et les éducateurs: essai sur la fortune des idées pédagogiques de Jean-Jacques Rousseau en France et en Europe au XVIIIe siècle*, thèse de Doctorat, université Paris IV, 1990.

[12] See E. Badinter, *L'amour en plus*, Le livre de Poche, 2001.

[13] See Philippe Ariès, *L'enfant et la vie familiale sous l'ancien régime*, Paris, Points Seuil 2003.

[14] *L'enfant chéri au Siècle des lumières. Après l'Émile* Catalogue de l'exposition, édition musée-promenade de Marly-le-Roi, Louveciennes, 2003.

As it discussed the utility of the Catholic or Protestant churches[15], *L'Emile* was forbidden by the Parliament of Paris a few days after its publication. Rousseau had to go into exile in Switzerland. The council of Geneva was no more tolerant, and for eight years, Rousseau became a hunted man.

On another level, the debates that Rousseau aroused provide a reflection that has not lost its interest in the present: they involve major questions, such as the mechanisms of cognition, the innate and the acquired, imagination and creativity, equality between individuals, and education for freedom. Rousseau's principles of education remain strongly debated in France, and are at stake in various battles over the reforms of school programs: the main dogma of «pedagogism» is to eliminate elitism and competition, and build an individual educative itinerary for each pupil with advices from an educator. "I teach my pupil a very difficult knowledge […], it is the art of being ignorant" Rousseau wrote[16]. Of course this is a witty paradox, but to what extent can this really be an educational program?

According to French philosopher Dominique Lecourt, «The struggle against elitism is conducted in the name of equality, but to the benefit of a misleading egalitarianism (...) The vehement criticism of authority implied by the relationship between master and pupil also affects all institutions in society, one after the other. These same people advocate for the child's free development: he must invent his path for himself. The school is assigned the aim of acquiring, not knowledge, but only skills: know-how and *savoir-être*.» Lecourt concludes: "The theses of *Emile* have invaded our schools, but it is wrong to believe that they represent the philosophy of the Enlightenment. One has only to read a few pages of Rousseau's

---

[15] cf. E*mile*, book 4, "La profession de foi du *vicaire savoyard*".
[16] *Emile*, book II.

Discours sur les sciences et les arts to see that Rousseau is not a man of the Enlightenment»[17].

The lack of access to abstract knowledge and especially science has been underlined as a major fault in Rousseau's principles; Diderot, on the contrary, shows deep, enthusiastic faith in the effectiveness of education, in the benefits of scientific learning and of social refinement. He refutes Rousseau's paradoxes about the pernicious effects of knowledge: "Far from corrupting, science softens characters, illuminates duties, eliminates or hides vices. I would dare to assume that progress of morality followed the progress of clothes from the beast skins to silk stuff"[18].

Another controversial issue in *Emile* is the part played by gender biases and concepts about girls' education. The education of Sophie, Emile's ideal wife, is presented in Book V: Sophie is mainly trained to sawing, making lace and cooking. «All the education of women must be relative to men» explains Rousseau, as he suggests that what Sophie learns about religion, art and the world is only acquired under the guidance of her husband. One can regret Rousseau's lack of imagination and strong biases regarding girls' education[19], and more generally on women in society, especially during a period – the French Enlightenment – when women started being involved in intellectual and social life and playing important roles in the public sphere[20].

---

[17] Dominique Lecourt, Introduction to François Xavier Bellamy, *Sur l'avenir de l'enseignement*, Les carnets des dialogues du matin, Institut Diderot, September 2016.

[18] Diderot, *Plan for a Russian University* (1775).

[19] Claude Habib, *Le Consentement amoureux: Rousseau, les femmes et la cité*, Paris, Hachette 1998; Victor G. Wexler "Made for Man's Delight": Rousseau as Antifeminist , *The American Historical Review*, Vol. 81, No. 2 (Apr., 1976), pp. 266-291.

[20] Roland BUNNEL et Catherine Rubinger (éd.): *Femmes savantes* et *femmes d'esprit. Women Intellectuals of the French Eighteenth Century*. New York, Peter Lang, 1994. See for example J. P. Zinsser, *La Dame D'esprit: A Biography of the Marquise Du Châtelet* – Viking, New York, 2006.

III – Bettering humanity through sensitivity Rousseau's ideas on Music

For Rousseau, sensitivity is the key to personal happiness and to human intercommunication. This is why music, which originally conveys feelings and emotion, is, in his eyes, another key to the improvement of humanity.

Even above being a philosopher, Rousseau was proud to entitle himself a musician. It is as a musician he came to Paris in 1742 and first hoped to gain success. It is as a music copyist he earned his living for a long part of his life. Music is according to him a means to reconnect with the roots of the human language and psyche, it exalts all the richness of human sensitivity.

Rousseau's *Essai sur l'origine des langues (Essay on the origin of languages*[21]*)* was first published in 1781, although it was probably written in the same period as the *Discours sur l'origine de l'inégalité.* In it, Rousseau proposed his own version of the origin and nature of the human language, in which he opposed in particular the ideas of another 18th century philosopher, Etienne de Condillac[22]. For Rousseau language is born form emotion, passion, seduction. It is the expression of original human sensitivity. Contrary to Condillac who defended the idea that language is born of needs, as a human «institution», Rousseau held in his *Essay* that «the origin of language is not due to the first needs of men; it would be absurd if the cause which separates them could be the means which unites them. « For Jean-Jacques, language is innate: it finds its origin in instincts and passions. «It is neither hunger nor thirst, but love, hatred, pity, and anger that initiates the first vocal expressions.»

---

[21] Jean-Jacques Rousseau, *The First and Second Discourses Together with the Replies to Critics; and, Essay on the Origin of Languages*, Harper and Row (1986).

[22] E. B. de Condillac, *Essai sur l'Origine des Connaissances humaines* Paris, 1746.

Condillac conceived that the first exchanges were gestures and screams, even before articulated language, and that the linguistic sign is arbitrary. Rousseau on the contrary imagines that expressive forms are the source of language: songs, cries of joy, of pain and anger... Onomatopoeia are associated with gestures, then come interjections, which will then develop into words and sentences. Music – that is, for Rousseau, voice, melody and singing – is the true expression of « nature ». Singing is the natural and original expression of affects and passions, and may well be the origin of the human language. Love songs of young people around the fountains would be this first language, and desire would be the primary motivation for speech.

"In arid places where water could only be found in wells, it was necessary to meet around them, or at least to agree on their use. This must have been the origin of societies and languages in hot countries. There were formed the first links of families, there happened meetings between both sexes.

Girls came to fetch water for the household, while young men came to water their herds (…) They arrived in haste, and left with regret. (…) Under the old oaks, an ardent youth forgot by degrees its ferocity... While striving to be heard, they learned to explain. There were made the first feasts, feet leaped with joy, the eager gesture was no longer sufficient, voice accompanied him with passionate accents; pleasure and desire, confounded together, were felt at once; there was finally the true cradle of the peoples; and from the pure crystal of fountains came forth the first fires of love"[23].

This is strongly linked with Rousseau's ideas on music[24]. Rousseau held that only a melodic line is true to nature, because it imitates the flow

---

[23] J.-J. Rousseau, *Essay*, Chapter X.

[24] Colm Kiernan, "Rousseau and Music in the French Enlightenment", *French Studies*, Volume XXVI, Issue 2, 1 April 1972, Pages 156-165.

of the human vocal emission. Therefore, harmony (the superposition of several musical sounds in chords) is "degenerate" music, it is unnatural – in particular because it must be written. Rousseau engaged in a strong polemic with Jean-Philippe Rameau, who was, in addition to being one of the French great composers of the time, the author of a major *Treatise of Harmony* (1722). According to Rousseau, Lully's and Rameau's operas are only boring, as they are too complicated and cerebral, whereas Italian opera, which has kept its melodic character, is able to speak to one's heart. The so-called «querelle des Bouffons»[25], between supporters of French opera and supporters of Italian opera, in which Rousseau took an active part, developed in a strong polemic after the staging of Pergolesi's *La Serva padrona* at the Royal Academy of Music in Paris, in 1752.

In his own musical compositions – namely his opera L*e Devin du Village,* first performed in October 1752 at Fontainebleau – Rousseau tried to bring innovations to this musical genre, in particular by including recitative and pantomime. In his songs, gathered under the title *Consolations des misères de ma vie* – Rousseau aimed to retrieve the simplicity and sensitivity of original singing.

Conclusion

It was a commonplace, in his time, to argue that Rousseau's ideas only carry his personal contradictions. There are certainly faults and biases in some aspects of Rousseau's thinking, but these do not seem to invalidate his major theoretical insights[26]. Rousseau's ideas about

---

[25] Andrea Fabiano. *La «Querelle des Bouffons» dans la vie culturelle française du XVIIIe siècle*. Paris, France. CNRS éditions, 2005.

[26] See Claude Lévi-Strauss, *Jean-Jacques Rousseau fondateur des sciences de l'homme*, Leçon donnée à l'Université Ouvrière de Genève dans le cadre du 250e anniversaire de la naissance de Jean-Jacques Rousseau (1962).

bettering humanity were based on the principles of human natural freedom and perfectibility. His concept of human improvement on the social and personal levels is deeply rooted in a political and ethical vision. Rousseau is a man of the Enlightenment but he is also a pre-Romantic, who made sensitivity the key to moral («pity» is the basic social link), the way to social improvement and to personal happiness (moral and religious consciousness, love, sensitivity to others).

Rousseau's ideas on politics, education and music are interesting to us because they strongly contrast with attempts to impose "from the outside" authoritarian criteria for "improving" humanity, of which episodes of recent history provide dismal examples, from eugenism to WWII's Nazi atrocities. The principles Rousseau outlined may also be valuable today for thinking critically, for example, the myths of "transhumanism" in today's world[27]. Rousseau's lesson is that our ability to progress and to gain freedom is in our hands and in our will, individually as well as collectively.

---

[27] See Nicolas Le Dévédec, «De l'humanisme au post-humanisme: les mutations de la perfectibilité humaine», *Revue du MAUSS permanente*, 21 décembre 2008 [on line] http://www.journaldumauss.net/spip.php?article444.

The contribution of British atheist reformers in the nineteenth Century

Jean-Patrick Connerade

This article summarises the role played by British atheist thinkers of the nineteenth century, most notably the early romantics clustering around Shelley, the Satanist Byron and the constitutional reformer Jeremy Bentham to the development of the modern democratic society which exists in Western Europe today. The origin of their thinking, rooted in the Industrial Revolution which developed around the Lancashire mills is described. The consequences were far-reaching, extending from social reform to political innovations, freedom movements, reforms of the judicial system, the birth of modern socialism and artistic influences which extended from an ecological strain in the poetry of the Romantic period to anti-science propaganda and the anti-science gothic novel Frankenstein. *e-mail: jean-patrick@connerade.com*

1.1 Introduction

When considering the contribution made by atheists to reforming society and establishing rules to guide people's actions, one should always bear in mind that there is something almost heroic about an atheist displaying moral principles. One can at least be sure that he is not in any way motivated by the expectation of some kind of reward in his afterlife. The atheist moralist is a remarkable animal indeed, an exotic species well-deserving of study in times such as our own, in which religions sometimes even threaten to lead us astray and moral standards are often said to be fast declining.

British atheist thinkers played a very important intellectual and reformist role during the nineteenth century. However, with the obvious exception of Darwin, they are in large part ignored, both in the UK and overseas, principally for two reasons. First, they were pioneers, far ahead of reformist thinking elsewhere in Europe at that time. Despite many social upheavals on the Continent, the public there was not yet ready to consider certain fundamental changes in the fabric of society whereas, in Great Britain, there was an increasing awareness amongst many intellectuals that changes were on their way which could not be resisted. Second, their views were completely rejected by the British establishment, whose brand of moderate parliamentarian conservatism was regarded as having triumphed at the battle of Waterloo. Nothing spurs on revolutionary thinking as effectively than being rejected by what innovators perceive as a rigid and inflexible establishment at a time when the social framework is undergoing major upheaval.

1.2 The pressures on British society due to the Indusrial Revolution

The role of the atheist thinkers in the evolution of British and European societies was almost subterranean and the strand of thought they represent is still considered alien to British values by many citizens of the United Kingdom to this day. Great Britain, by and large, is a very conservative nation with highly inventive industrial and maritime traditions. The result is a tension due to the introduction of technical innovations into a rigid framework. This can lead to the emergence of unwanted change, as dictated by the laws of the market, in spite of opposition by established industrial magnates or even by the workforce itself. Examples of the latter include the Peterloo massacre and the Luddite movement. Change may appear somewhat erratic in such a society, since it appears in response to hidden pressures which are rarely made explicit. The merit of the much misunderstood British atheist thinkers was their attempt to formulate or give explicit voice to these hidden tensions, as a result of which they invented a reformist trend we would recognise today as an early form of socialism.

The birth of the Industrial Revolution in England is attributable in large part to the revocation of the Edict of Nantes by King Louis the fourteenth of France, who thus expelled from his country the protestant population known as *Huguenots*. By and large, the Huguenots were educated and adventurous people, who brought with them an innovative and inventive spirit as well as a deep knowledge of the techniques involved in cloth making. They also, because of their continental roots, remained well-informed of social and political changes which subsequently occurred in France and elsewhere. Huguenots had emigrated to other protestant countries, which included Prussia and they were present in large numbers in Berlin.

1.3 The contrast between Great Britain and the Continent of Europe in the nineteenth century

The situation elsewhere in Europe, where all forms of change were spontaneously theorised and immediately assumed a philosophical dimension, was a completely different one. Change in this environment was not due to hidden forces. They were apparent for all to see in the French Revolution.

This kind of social evolution was of course also driven by economic forces, but not the same ones. The Industrial Revolution, on the continent of Europe, had not yet occurred. Technological development there was lagging far behind the British Isles and so the context was very different. Seen from overseas, British or 'Anglo-Saxon' society was ushering in welcome or more often unwelcome change ahead of their own development. While intellectuals may have understood what was going on, such change was still irrelevant to most of the population.

Basically, one can consider that two different forms of progress were at work, one on each side of the Channel, which created a time warp between different parts of Europe. This was particularly the case in the eighteenth and throughout the nineteenth centuries: in its beginnings especially, but even some fifty to one hundred years later, the Industrial Revolution remained a peculiarly British phenomenon. This fact had a profound influence both on European development as a whole and eventually also on Western Art. The changes which eventually came about all over Europe were not simply the result of military conflict. They can be likened to a tidal wave which swept down from Lancashire, progressing fast through Prussia and Central Europe and, somewhat more slowly, through France and the 'Latin' nations whose economies remained more agricultural for a very long time.

This aspect of development was also driven by geography. Some of the most fertile plains in Europe are to be found in the area of France known as Beauce. It is proverbial in French to say that the harvests of Beauce can feed the whole of Europe, and so the economic pressure to industrialise was not felt in France as strongly as it was elsewhere. In fact, the French economy retained a dominant agricultural component until fairly recently, the evolution towards an industrial nation having been achieved during the thirty years from 1945 to 1975 when the country restructured itself after the Second World War.

Since social change in Europe was spearheaded largely by the French Revolution and was largely opposed by the British establishment in the eighteenth and nineteenth centuries, one sees that the pressures on society were rather different on both sides of the channel.

1.4 Intellectual change in Great Britain: Romanticism and Bonapartism

The first aspect of intellectual change, which goes largely unrecognised, is that British atheism in this period is not merely the eccentric creed of a few isolated individuals. In fact, it is a political and intellectual movement, like many others of its time, resulting from the progress of science. It connects very closely to the two most powerful influences at work at this point in history, namely Romanticism in the arts on one hand and innovative technology on the other. In order to appreciate its revolutionary political stance, one must also understand the complex relationship between British Romanticism and the Bonapartist opposition in Britain, elements of which survived for at least a generation after 1815, as well as the love-hate relationship British poetry entertained with science and technology, deriving its new strength from the social and ecological consequences of early industrialisation. The poets predate the philosophers in their disgust for industrialisation. Karl Marx and George Orwell come a good deal later than Shelley and the lake-ist poets but follow in this trend.

The reason why Great Britain played such a crucial role in this period as compared with other countries in Europe rests on two fundamental realities. First, its external policy as a maritime and colonial superpower was designed to preserve commercial interests and the social *status quo* in other countries of Europe by all available military means during the Napoleonic wars. Second, as an unwelcome consequence of its considerable advance over other European nations in industrial power and, therefore, it was the first nation in

Europe to be faced with industrial wastelands, mass poverty due to mechanisation and the sudden emergence of an urban proletariat. Seen from this perspective, one can understand that thinkers such as Karl Marx were convinced that their own impending social revolution should first occur in Britain, before any other European nation. What they underestimated was the resilience of the British establishment and the tight control exercised by its ruling class in mobilising the forces of insular nationalism to isolate the people from foreign influences and moderate the emergence of what they painted as dangerous foreign ideas.

The paradox of an industrially progressive nation with a reactionary social structure was precisely the opposite of the mainstream situation elsewhere in Europe, where industry generally lagged behind rapid social change due to political instability prior to industrialisation.

1.5 Bourgeois versus revolutionary Romantics

For all the reasons given above, the Romantic movement in the UK developed differently from the German, French or Italian schools. From the outset, it split into two separate strands which reflect a division within British society, where the consequences of the French Revolution had been averted. On the one hand were the rabid rebels (Byron, Shelley, Godwin, Bentham, Erasmus Darwin and their friends) fundamentally opposed to the establishment of the day, whose sympathies lay with the Napoleonic adventure. On the other were the 'bourgeois Romantics', persons of social substance and reassuring conservatism, mainly from the Manchester school (Wordsworth, Coleridge, De Quincey and the Lake poets) whose only possible quarrel with their political and economic masters was the terrible smoke produced by burning large quantities of coal. While they produced some early examples of 'ecological poetry', the Manchester group nonetheless relied on industry to produce wealth and were happy enough with the kind of compromise which consisted in planting a curtain of trees in front of unsightly factories and withdrawing amongst themselves in a gentlemanly huddle to the preserved countryside of the Lake District made fashionable by William Wordsworth.

The conflict between the two schools was ideologically profound. The Manchester poets were pretty conventional in all their principles. They seldom expressed religious views, but were basically Anglicans or Protestants. Even the opium eaters amongst them had found a comfortable place as established artists in a well-regulated society. In contrast, such wild characters as Byron, Shelley and their friends were far more radical in outlook and some carried their opinions and lifestyle to the point of provocation, obliging them to emigrate and become, in a sense, European refugees from what they regarded as British bigotry. Byron, for example, had a visceral hatred of Coleridge, often expressed in his correspondence, as well as a hatred of science he made every effort to instill into the mind of Mary Shelley.

1.6 Lord Byron, Godwin, the Darwins and the Shelleys

The classic example of the British atheist in this period is of course Percy Bysshe Shelley, whose declared atheism is alleged to be the reason he was 'sent down' from Oxford University (the true reason is probably more complex and may well have concerned his love of chemistry, leading to random explosions and bad smells in the corridors of St Johns College). Once he had appeared in London and joined the group around the atheist philosopher and publisher Godwin (which included Erasmus Darwin, the grandfather of Charles Darwin), it was inevitable that he should come into contact with Byron, who was naturally attracted towards a young man with such a radical philosophical stance. William Godwin, the author of *Political Justice* (perhaps the earliest modern treatise to expound the principles of Anarchism) was Shelley's publisher and printed a treatise on social change by Shelley which is regarded as probably the first Socialist pamphlet produced in Britain.

Byron was not at all a regular atheist. He was what one should properly call a Satanist, i.e. a person fundamentally opposed to God, but quite happy to deal with the devil if only he could be summoned and persuaded to appear. His ambition was to personify the 'bad Lord' and even his famous limp was something he was proud to share with Lucifer as a consequence of his fall from heaven. However, he saw an atheist like Shelley the poet as a welcome friend and ally in his general fight against the establishment. He considered the duke of Wellington as a murderer and used his social status as the Lord Byron to tell him so to his face. Amongst his more amusing eccentricities, he decided to change his own Christian name to Napoleon and wrote a highly entertaining letter to the House of Lords informing them of this bizarre decision, pointing out that, henceforth, he would sign all his communications 'NB' with the same initials as Bonaparte, which would allow him also to continue adding in further paragraphs to his letters as "*Nota Bene*" as he felt the urge.

When Shelley fled Britain carrying off not just one but actually both of Godwin's daughters together, his behaviour was considered so dreadful that he ended up an exile on the Continent. Lord Byron was in the same position, having had a daughter by his own sister and being consequently ostracised by high society despite his noble birth.

So, when they met up in Switzerland, together with the Godwin daughters and Byron's strange personal secretary Polidori, they probably formed the most infamous and celebrated group of intellectuals anywhere in Europe at the time, contributing greatly to the dark reputation of the Romantic movement as a whole. It is in Switzerland that they developed the gothic novel, and that Mary Shelley began to put together her *Frankenstein*, which was to be the emblematic anti-science book for many generations to come and is still used to feed hostility towards scientific research in many circles around the world today. It is worth noting that Mary Shelley, as a child, had heard Erasmus Darwin talk about his experiments on passing electrical currents (recently discovered by Volta and Galvani) through the legs of dead frogs and may even have witnessed some of them. The true motivation for her own tale is complex, as she was torn between Shelley, who loved science, and Byron, who hated it. While she remained, as far as we know, faithful to the poet Shelley, the influence Byron had on her inner self was huge, as one can tell from the preface to the second edition of *Frankenstein* (the one she wrote herself: the preface to the first edition was actually written by her husband) and from all the other books she subsequently wrote, in each one of which Byron appears under different disguises.

1.7 Jeremy Bentham, the British Atheist Philosopher, and Voltaire, the French Deist

Although the poet Shelley had ambitions as a social reformer, the true innovator in this field was not him but Jeremy Bentham. He is often referred to as 'the English Voltaire' but in reality was quite different and the difference between the two reflects all the social differences between both sides of the Channel at the time. Although Voltaire came to England for a short stay motivated in large part by the need to stay away from the French Monarchy for a while, owing to his controversial writings, he remained, in style, in behaviour and even in his opinions, a pure product of the French upper class court civilization. He was made well aware of the difference in nature between Britain as a merchant nation and France as an agricultural autocracy and even wrote his *Lettres sur les Anglais*

(Letters on the English) in an effort to inform his friends at home that there existed another, sometimes strange, society which was based on different rules, on a different social structure and had developed different art forms from those of the Continent of Europe. But fundamentally, his thinking and his style were not changed by this discovery.

While Voltaire was opposed to priesthood and conventional religion, he never challenged the notion of the existence of a God or some kind of supreme being. He famously commented that he could not imagine the existence of such a piece of clockwork as the Universe without there being a clockmaker.

Jeremy Bentham, of course, comes later than Voltaire and only knew about him through reading his works. He was undoubtedly influenced by Voltaire's ideas about an ideal form of government, but the influence stops there. Jeremy Bentham was a true atheist and, because of his more extreme position, wanted to re-visit all the fundamentals of social construction and, in particular, the whole basis of education., from a different point of view. He was also a much more practical person He was a co-founder of University College London which, through his influence and that of his circle, became the first institution of higher education in Great Britain with no religious connotation whatsoever.

1.8 Jeremy Bentham the Reformer

Amongst the important reforms attributed to Bentham was the idea of opening the doors of the University to female students, which occurred at an early date at University College London. Initially, they were only allowed in as free auditors but were not registered as full-time students, Soon, however, Bentham argued they should also be allowed to sit examinations and obtain qualifications, which was an amazing and controversial step. This, without doubt, is the pioneer spirit which attracted many brilliant female writers to reside in the district, laying foundations for a group later renowned as *the Bloomsbury set*.

By training and family tradition, Bentham was a lawyer, although he was so shocked by what he regarded as immoral profiteering by the barristers of his time that he never practised and, instead, resolved to devote his efforts to penal and constitutional reform. Soon, he was to branch out into many areas of philosophy and sociology, much inspired by the ideas emerging at the onset of the French Revolution. Indeed, he became very well regarded by the early revolutionaries and (a bit like Thomas Paine) traveled to France and was even granted honorary French citizenship in 1792.

However, he soon detected that Bonaparte would seek to become an autocrat, and he rejected this aspect of the French Revolution. Regarding social reform, he was quite practical in outlook and wanted to follow ideas through all the way to their application. Thus, he became attracted by the idea of designing the perfect architecture for ideal prisons and penal establishments (the *panopticum*) allowing permanent surveillance in order to reform the spirit of its inmates. Probably, they would not have appreciated all his ideas, which were more than a little 'Big Brother' in style, but some of the proposals in the *panopticum* were actually implemented and, for better or for worse, have probably influenced the design and development of gaols to this day.

1.9 Bentham, colonial rule and independence movements

Because of his interest in drafting modern constitutions for newly independent countries and his strong belief that, like North America, all the colonies should be emancipated, he was consulted by countries which had already achieved, or which hoped to achieve, independence. This idea, of course, is rooted in the French Revolution with its declaration of the right of peoples of the world to choose freely their own form of government. However, Bentham wished to apply this principle, which most of the French revolutionaries, despite the fine words, did not.

As a result, he became involved in the independence movements of Latin America and gave early advice on their constitutions. Most notably, he was approached by the nationalist movement seeking Greek independence from Ottoman rule. In response to their solicitations, he assembled like-minded colleagues and founded the *Committee for Greek Independence*, which met on several occasions at the Anchor pub in London. However, as his own radical views had not much impact on British society, he had the adventurous idea of contacting Lord Byron and convincing him to join this Committee, which the famous poet embraced with enthusiasm. The manifesto they all signed, calling for Greek independence, was published in the *Morning Chronicle* and what followed is an important page of European history.

The British Government was staunchly opposed to the idea of Greek Independence, no doubt because it had a colonial agenda with the aim of 'inheriting' useful islands after the demise of the Ottoman Empire. At this point, seeing an independence movement spontaneously taking shape, it went so far as to threaten British Subjects with prison should they venture to serve under any foreign flag. By this point, Byron had emigrated to Venice where he was living with the countess Guiccioli, but he was so irritated with the lack of concern of many fellow citizens and by what he regarded as criminal negligence of human rights by his own country that he decided to put his own considerable fortune and, indeed, his life in the service of this cause. He rented and equipped at his own expense a military ship, the *Hercules*, hired sailors and soldiers and famously sailed from Livorno to Cephalos and Missolonghi, where he met his death at the beginning of the fight for freedom of the Greek people. This celebrated event, of course, attracted comment worldwide and the admiration of such people as Johann Wolfgang Goëthe, a lifelong friend of Byron. But one should not forget that Jeremy Bentham was the one who pressed politically for international action, in a form of idealism comparable to the spirit of the international volunteers engaged in the Spanish Civil war.

1.10 Bentham, Atheist Morality and Social Reform

A particular feature of Bentham's thinking was his pursuit of a modern dream one might call *atheist morality*. As a disciple of the Swiss thinker Claude-Adrien Helvétius, he was convinced that his proposals were not in any way idealistic, but entirely practical. Indeed, he chose to describe his own philosophical movement as utilitarianism. There is something endearing and almost eccentric in everything he attempted. His form of rationalism tends permanently towards a paradox. Indeed, he would have enjoyed George Bernard Shaw's definition of a paradox as 'truth standing on its head in order to attract attention'.

Based on principles originally due to Helvétius (who strongly influenced Stendhal's *de l'Amour*), Bentham developed a very interesting theory about what makes people happy or unhappy. He halled it the *felicific calculus*. The idea was to measure scientifically the degree of pleasure or of revulsion generated by our actions. Doesn't this remind you, nowadays, of the King of Bouthan and his Gross National Happiness (GNH) index?

Bentham defined seven criteria as follows:

1. A lasting pleasure has more value than a short one.
2. An intense form of pleasure has more value than a weak one.
3. Certainty provides more pleasure than doubt.
4. Proximity brings more pleasure than realisation in the distant future.
5. A pleasure shared with others has more value than if it is individual.

6. A pleasure leading to many more is better than one which occurs only once.

7. Pleasure leading to no bad consequences is superior to than all others.

In Bentham's theory, the most moral action is the one which satisfies as many as possible of these seven criteria. Bentham was totally opposed to Rousseau over the notion of a Social Contract as a compromise whereby individuals sacrifice some of their aspirations in order to benefit from advantages only an organised state can provide. According to Bentham, the state should be there only to promote the collective happiness of its citizens. This means that new laws must be designed to enhance the index computed by his felicific calculus.

This leads Bentham to a number of very modern and radical suggestions, for example:

(i) the State must ensure the safety of all its citizens;

(ii) property must be protected;

(iii) the State should guarantee a universal minimum wage;

(iv) the State should foster economic growth;

(v) the State should favour population growth;

(vi) to avoid inequality, riches should be redistributed via an inheritance tax.

1.11 Some other political consequences of Bentham's system

Other consequences are perhaps less obvious but were also derived by Bentham from his system. They contrast sharply with the views of the British establishment in his time, but are not far removed from what we would accept today. He argued that, by construction, monarchies, dictatorships and oligarchies only maximise the happiness of a small minority of citizens. For Bentham, the ideal society must therefore be democratic. This principle, however, he did not carry as far as we do. He was in favour of a limited degree of democracy, depending on an assessment of social position based on the ability to pay a wealth tax, so as to induce a sense of responsibility on the part of voters. In his pursuit of justice, Bentham (remarkably) also spoke up for the rights of homosexuals and is believed to have written the first pamphlet on this subject in the English language.

Fig. 1.1. Jeremy Bentham (Portrait by Henry William Pickergill)

1.12 A brief assessment of Bentham's place in his century

As I remarked initially, Jeremy Bentham, as a philosopher, is not remembered as quite the equal of Voltaire or Rousseau, but this is perhaps in some ways unfair. His influence on European society was far greater than is realised. The pursuit of happiness in the way he formulated it is close to the contemporary notion of 'well-being' and he was amongst the first to seek an almost scientific basis for social justice, which can be viewed as laying the foundations of the Social Sciences. He championed decolonisation and the equality of sexes. He also influenced philosophical thought with the help of his friends and allies who included John Stuart Mill and Adam Smith. It is in some ways strange that his motivations as a reformist were idealistic but expressed themselves through the doctrine of utilitarianism. However, this paradox is not far removed from the principles of what we call today *sustainable development* which are in some ways idealistic but seek justification in the scientific basis of global warming. Through this tension, Benthams contribution is very relevant today. He would have sided against some contemporary economic theories which leave aside any form of idealism, just as he sided against the legal system of his time which he considered immoral in its practice.

Bentham is the most accomplished and influential of the British atheist philosophers of this period in history. He created a circle gravitating around the newly founded University College of which he was a founding member. His lifelong friendship with Erasmus Darwin, another notable atheist; is undoubtedly one reason why Charles Darwin applied and was appointed to a chair at University College.

Bentham's complete works were published in Brussels in 1845.

1.13 Bentham the eccentric

Bentham had inherited enough wealth to live comfortably in Westminster, and he bequeathed his fortune to the college on condition that his embalmed body should attend all future meetings of its governing Committee. This was implemented, and the phrase 'Jeremy came; but said nothing' was added at the end of the minutes of each meeting as proof that the conditions of Bentham's will had been respected. Fairly recently, Bentham's head fell off during one of these meetings and a bad smell spread in the room. A Professor of Medicine suggested that Bentham's continued presence might present some health problems for members of the Committee, so it was decided to leave Bentham on his wheelchair in the glass case where he is kept and add only the sentence to the minutes, except perhaps for very important meetings.

1.13 Conclusion

The British atheists of the nineteenth century are a very remarkable group of intellectuals, whose action was at the same time social, scientific and political. It is also strongly connected with Romanticism and with the Industrial Revolution. As such, it would deserve much further study and its influence overseas deserves to be analysed. At the time, Great Britain was unique in its colonial power, its industrial wealth and also in the pressures they induced on its social structure, which is the underlying cause of the emergence of such an original group of thinkers. It is arguable that they were ahead of other avant-garde European movements of their time and that, in fact, they led the way forward towards social reform in Europe after the end of the Napoleonic wars. In order to appreciate many facets of their creative spirit, ranging from the arts to the sciences and over a wide range of social and political innovations, one should consider their movement as a whole, which gives a clearer view of its importance.

References

Bentham, Jeremy [1845]. *The Works of Jeremy Bentham, published under the Superintendence of his Executor*, John Bowring (Edinburgh: William Tait, 1838-1843). 11 vols. <http://oll.libertyfund.org/titles/1925>
    Note: a new critical edition of the works and correspondence of Jeremy Bentham (1748-1832) is being prepared and published under the supervision of the Bentham Committee of University College London. In spite of his importance as jurist, philosopher, and social scientist, and leader of the Utilitarian movement, the only previous edition of his works the original 1845 edition is rather incomplete. Eight volumes of his *Collected Works*, five of correspondence, and three of writings on jurisprudence, appeared between 1968 and 1981 published by the Athlone Press. Further volumes in the series were since published by the Oxford University Press. The overall plan and principles of the edition are set out in the General Preface to *The Correspondence of Jeremy Bentham*, vol. 1 is the first volume of the *Collected Works* published so far.

Bentham, Jeremy [1789]. *An Introduction to the Principles of Morals and Legislation*, Bentham's best-known work, is a classic text in modern philosophy and jurisprudence. Iit contains the important statements of the foundations of utilitarian philosophy and a pioneering study of crime and punishment, both of which are central to contemporary debates in moral and political philosophy, economics, and law. A definitive edition has been edited by the Bentham scholars J. H. Burns and H. L. A. Hart. The introductory essay by Hart contains an analysis of Bentham's principle of utility, theory of action, and an account of the relationship he developed between law and morality. A new introduction by the Bentham scholar F. Rosen, written for the Clarendon Paperback edition, provides a survey of Bentham's main ideas and an extensive bibliographical study of recent critical work on Bentham. Professor Rosen's essay also contains a new analysis of the principle of utility in Bentham's philosophy as compared with its use by Hume and J. S. Mill.

Byron, George Gordon, Lord. *Letters and Journals* Edited by Leslie A. Marchand (11 volumes) published by John Murray 1973 onwards, London, Becclées and Colchester (complete edition).

Chaunes, M. [2013]. *Ecology and Creationism in European Culture*, page 9 of *Science meets Poetry 3*, Proceedings of the ESOF2012, Forum (Edited by J.-P.

Connerade and I. McGovern) published by EuroScience (Strasbourg) ISBN 978-1481951005

Godwin, William [1793]. *Enquiry Concerning Political Justice and its Influence on Morals and Happiness* (Penguin Classics), London Paperback, 2015, Introduction by Isaac Kramnick.

Shelley, Mary [1818]. *Frankenstein or the Modern Prometheus,* Guild Publishing, London, 1980, St Edmundsbury Press Bury, St Edmunds Suffolk.

Stendhal [1853]. *De l'amour,* Lévy frères, Paris.

Voltaire [1733]. *Lettres philosophiques, ou Lettres sur les Anglais,* (published in English the same year under the title *Letters concerning the English nation*), the Voltaire Foundation launched both online, see https://voltairefoundation.wordpress.com/tag/lettres-sur-les-anglais/

The Vienna Circle and its place in the history of positivism

Annette B. Vogt

The history of positivism as a philosophical theory goes back to the 18th century when the French philosopher Auguste Comte (1798-1857) published his work. Among the most important thinkers to develop the concept of positivism were the French philosopher Émile Durkheim (1858-1917) and the Austrian scholar Ernst Mach (1838-1916). In the early 20th century the capital Vienna became a center for discussions on positivism as well as for the further developments, also known as neo-positivism. The „Vienna Circle" became a synonym for this development, when philosophers and mathematicians, physicists, economists and sociologists discussed together and against each other. Because of the rise of Nazism, from 1933 on in Germany, and from 1938 on in Austria, most of these important scientists, philosophers and scholars who were representatives of the „Vienna Circle" or who were involved in the development of the concept of an „unified science" had to go into exile. Thus the USA became the new home country of this philosophical discipline.

In the present paper I'll discuss some of these aspects. First, I sketch out the definitions of positivism as a philosophical theory, and the later developments, known as logical positivism, neo-positivism, and post-positivism. Then, the history of the famous „Vienna Circle" is described, from 1907 until its abrupt end in 1938. It will be explained what was called the „Vienna Circle", when it happened, who were the members, what were the contexts and disciplines, which results and outcomes were made, and what were the influences. And a special aspect will be described, the fate, the circumstances, and the aims of the publication of Richard von Mises (1883-1953), his book „Positivism. A Study in human understanding".

The „Vienna Circle" wasn't only one circle, it had a kind of sub-circles, there was an inner circle, located in Vienna, and there were outer circles, the periphery. Between these circles one could reconstruct the network among them. A small group of its representatives was working in Berlin, especially the philosopher Hans Reichenbach (1891-1953) and the mathematician and aerodynamicist Richard von Mises. Furthermore, R. von Mises was a friend of the physicist and mathematician Philipp Frank (1884-1964) who was a member of the first circle in Vienna until 1912 when he became a professor in Prague. From 1912 to 1938 he was working at the German University in Prague, and he was called a „Machist". Philipp Frank was also a close friend of Albert Einstein (1879-1955). Philipp Frank later will become one of the editors of the book series „Library of unified science". In this series the book „Positivism. A Study in human understanding" by R. von Mises was published in 1939 as volume I.

The „Vienna Circle" today means not only the place, i. e. the town Vienna, but it means also the kind of distribution of knowledge, the kind of discussions, the exchange of knowledge and experiences, the debates between scholars from different disciplines, especially between the mathematicians and scientists on the one side and philosophers and social scientists on the other side. The „Vienna Circle", i. e. the way in which different scholars, the philosophers and social scientists, physicists and mathematicians, economists and sociologists, discussed together and against each other, became most famous in the period between 1918 and 1934/36. The debates and their outcomes – publications, the journal and the book series – played an important role in the history of philosophy as well as in the history of science. Whereas the ideal of „unified science" is still an open research question, the development of philosophy, sociology, and history of science was deeply influenced by the thinkers who belonged to the „Vienna Circle", to the inner circle as well as to the periphery.

Before we sketch out the three time periods of its history and describe the members of these groups who belonged for a shorter or longer time to the inner circle and the periphery we have to give some informations to trace back the roots of these discussions.

From positivism to logical positivism

Positivism is a philosophical theory where knowledge is based on natural phenomena, their properties and relations. It is based on empiricism, and empirical evidence is demanded. From the beginning, the theory was constructed against metaphysics and theology. Assuming that general laws are existing, one of the main hypotheses was then that general laws are existing in societies too. Whereas positivism was developed already in the 18th century, further steps were made in the 20th century, and logical positivism, neo-positivism and post-positivism are linked with positivism. The French philosophers Auguste Comte (1798-1857) and Émile Durkheim (1858-1917) played an important role in developing the philosophical theory called positivism.[1] The Austrian physicist Ernst Mach (1838-1916) was another important thinker who influenced not only the members of the „Vienna Circle" but also the history of philosophy and the history of science.[2] The slogan „Ordem e Progresso" became not only the „Leitmotiv" of positivist scholars, it is part of the flag of Brazil, and in Porto Alegre in Brazil exists a „Temple of Positivism".

---

[1] See Comte, Auguste. A General View of Positivism. Published first in 1848, an English version was published first in 1865. On Émile Durkheim see Lukes, Steven. Émile Durkheim, his life and work. A historical and critical study. Stanford: University Press, 1990.

[2] On Ernst Mach see Cohen, Robert S. (ed) Ernst Mach. Physicist and Philosopher. Amsterdam: Kluwer Academic Publishers, 1975.

Positivism as a philosophical theory was developed first in Europe, but later transfered to many other places.

The development of philosophy in Vienna after 1900 was closely linked with positivism and was also called logical positivism or logical empiricism. Discussing the role of the „Vienna Circle" one has to distinguish three time periods: the years 1907-1912, 1918-1924, and 1924-1936/38. From 1920 to 1933 a small group of representatives of the „Vienna Circle" was working at the Berlin University. In the broader public the „Vienna Circle" became better known in 1929 when the so-called „Manifesto" was published, an initiative of Otto Neurath (1882-1945), a political economist and one of the key figures in the history of this movement. Because of the Nazi's the fruitful discussions, the publications, and the whole development was ended abruptly, first in Germany from 1933 onwards, then from March 1938 onwards in Austria. Many members of the „Vienna Circle" had to go into exile, most of them escaped the Nazi persecution, and many of them took part in the further developments which followed in the USA.

Comparatively late the history of the „Vienna Circle" was re-discovered, meanwhile many books were published, on the history in general as well as on its famous members. The University of Vienna is proud now of this famous group. In 2015 an exhibition was organised, from May 20 until October 31, 2015 the exhibition „Der Wiener Kreis – The Vienna Circle – Exaktes Denken am Rand des Untergangs – Exact thinking in demented times" was shown in the main building of the University. The Austrian historian of science and philosophy Friedrich Stadler (b. 1951) has contributed enormously to the history of that circle. In 1997 he published his book on the Vienna Circle[3], in 1991 he

---

[3] See Stadler, Friedrich. Studien zum Wiener Kreis. Ursprung, Entwicklung und Wirkung des Logischen Empirismus im Kontext. Frankfurt am Main: Suhrkamp, 1997; English: The Vienna Circle. Studies in the Origins, Development, and Influence of Logical Empiricism. Wien and New York: Springer, 2001.

was the founder and since then the long-time director of the „Institute Vienna Circle" which became part of the Vienna University in 2011. This Institute publishes a Yearbook, from 1993 on the annual „Vienna Circle Lecture" takes place, and further research projects are dealing with different aspects and various members of the „Vienna Circle".[4] Thanks to the work of Friedrich Stadler and his colleagues we know today much more on the roots, the different views and statements of this development.[5] We know more about the members in the inner circle and the periphery, on their motivations and contributions to that development, on their impact on further directions like philosophy and logic of science, history of science, sociology of science, and science studies.

The Vienna Circle – time periods and places

In the history of the „Vienna Circle" one has to distinguish three time periods. The members of these meetings – the name „circle" was given later – met each other in the first years in coffee houses in Vienna. It is known that some scholars met between 1907 and 1912 in the coffee house Cafe Josephinum in Vienna, and the most famous participants in these years were the physicist Philipp Frank, the mathematician Hans Hahn (1879-1934), and the political economist and sociologist Otto Neurath. Philipp Frank became professor at the German University

---

[4] See the homepage of Friedrich Stadler with the link to „Wiener Kreis Gesellschaft" and here to the „Institute Vienna Circle"; here the annual lectures are listed and the research projects are described: *www.univie.ac.at/zeitgeschichte/friedrich-stadler/*

[5] See more recently Sigmund, Karl. Sie nannten sich der Wiener Kreis: Exaktes Denken am Rand des Untergangs. Heidelberg et al: Springer Spektrum, 2015 (2nd ed. 2018). English transl.. Exact Thinking in Demented Times. The Vienna Circle and the Epic Quest for the Foundations of Science. Basic: 2017.

of Prague in 1912, but he was always interested in the work and the discussions. Between 1918 and 1924 and 1924 and 1928 the second period took place, again the participants met in coffee houses, and there were different discussion circles with different members and groups of members.

During the third period, from 1928 to the late 1930s the members met in the rooms of the Mathematical Seminar of the Vienna University in Boltzmanngasse 5. The end of the „Vienna Circle" happened in three steps, first because of the political situation in Austria in 1934 and the death of Hans Hahn in the same year – one of the key figures from the beginning –, second the murder of Moritz Schlick in June 1936, and finally the take over (Anschluss) by the Nazi's in March 1938. Only during this third period the participants met in rooms of the University, and the name of the discussion group was partly the Schlick Circle (after Moritz Schlick). Furthermore, the Ernst Mach Society (Verein Ernst Mach) organised different meetings, and discussions. This third period was the most successful one. In 1929 the „Manifesto" was published, a journal was edited from 1930 onwards, a book series was planned, and six international conferences were organised from 1929 to 1938. Therefore, one could argue that the real „Vienna Circle" with regular meetings and discussions existed from 1924 until 1936 when Moritz Schlick was killed by a (Nazi) student.

The key figures of the „Vienna Circle" were, beside the physicist Philipp Frank (1884-1966) during the first period, the mathematician Hans Hahn (1879-1934), the political economist Otto Neurath (1882-1945) and the physicist and philosopher Moritz Schlick (1882-1936) who was killed on June 22 in 1936. From 1922 to 1934 he was the chair of philosophy at the University of Vienna. Only Hans Hahn and Moritz Schlick were professors at the University of Vienna, and some of their PhD students participated in the circle.

The Vienna Circle – the members

The „Vienna Circle" wasn't only one circle, there were also sub-circles, and there was an inner circle, located in Vienna, and there were outer circles, the periphery. Between these circles one could reconstruct the network. [repetition: this was said already above] One could distinguish three groups of members, the inner circle with all in all 18 scholars (among them two women), the periphery with all in all 17 scholars (among them four women), and four promoters or supporters, two British scholars and two US philosophers.

The four promoters were the British philosopher Alfred Jules Ayer (1910-1989), who became the promoter of logical positivism; the philosopher from the USA Charles W. (William) Morris (1901-1979), 1931-1947 professor of philosophy at the Chicago University, in 1934 he visited Europe, including Vienna, and he became one of the editors of the IEUS (International Encyclopedia of Unified Science) started in 1939 as „Library of unified science, book series"; the US philosopher Willard Van Orman Quine (1908-2000), who visited Europe 1932-1933 and also Vienna, he is regarded as one of the most influential philosophers, following the analytic philosophy tradition and supporting the logical positivist movement; and finally the British mathematician and economist Frank P. Ramsey (1903-1930), who was in 1924 in Vienna and who was a friend of Ludwig Wittgenstein (1889-1951) who is often mentioned as a member of the „Vienna Circle" but who belonged in reality to the periphery of the circle.

The 18 members of the inner circle were beside Moritz Schlick (1882-1936):[6]

---

[6] The names of the female members were marked bold to underline them; to give at least the basic information of the later fate of the members, i. e. their way into exile, the places of birth and death are given here too.

Gustav Bergmann (1906 Vienna – 1987 Iowa City),
Rudolf Carnap (1891 Ronsdorf/Wuppertal – 1970 Santa Monica/
    Calif.),
Herbert Feigl (1902 Reichenberg – 1988 USA),
Philipp Frank (1884 Vienna – 1966 Cambridge (Mass.)),
Kurt Gödel (1906 Brünn – 1978 Princeton),
Hans Hahn (1879-1934),
Olga Hahn-Neurath (1882 Vienna –1937 The Hague),
Béla Juhos (1901-1971),
Felix Kaufmann (1895 Vienna – 1949 New York),
Viktor Kraft (1880-1975),
Karl Menger (1902 Vienna – 1985 Highland Park, Ill.),
Richard von Mises (1883 Lemberg – 1953 Boston),
Otto Neurath (1882 Vienna – 22.12.1945 Oxford),
Rose Rand (1903 Lemberg – 1980 USA),
Josef Schächter (1901 Galicia – 1994 Haifa, Isr.),
Friedrich Waisman(n) (1896 Vienna – 1959 Oxford),
and Edgar Zilsel (1891 Vienna – 1944 Oakland, Calif.).

The 17 members of the periphery were:

Egon Brunswik (1903 Budapest –1955 Berkeley, Calif.),
Karl Bühler (1879 Meckesheim, Baden – 1963 Los Angeles),
Charlotte Bühler (1893 Berlin – 1974 Stuttgart),
Josef Frank (1885 Baden/Vienna – 1967 Stockholm),
Else Frenkel-Brunswik (1908 Lemberg – 1958 Berkeley, Calif.),
Heinrich Gomperz (1873 Vienna – 1942 Los Angeles),
Carl Gustav Hempel (1905 Orianienburg (Berlin) – 1997
    Princeton),
Eino Sakari Kaila (1890-1958), 1930 prof. of philosophy at the
    University Helsinki,

Hans Kelsen (1881 Prague – 1973 Berkeley),

Oskar Morgenstern (1902 Görlitz – 1977 Princeton),

Arne Naess (1912-2009), in 1939 prof. of philosophy at the University Oslo,

Ernest Nagel (1901 Slovakia – 1985 New York),

Hans Reichenbach (1891 Hamburg – 1953 Los Angeles),

Kurt Reidemeister (1893-1971), brother of

Marie Reidemeister-Neurath (1898-1986),

Alfred Tarski (orig. Alfred Teitelbaum) (1901 Warsaw – 1983 Berkeley), 1930 and 1935 in Vienna; and

Olga Taussky-Todd (1906 Olmütz – 1995 Pasadena, Calif.).

In contacts to some of the members but never belonging to the circle were the philosophers Ludwig Wittgenstein (1889 Vienna – 1951 Cambridge (UK)) and (Sir) Karl Popper (1902 Vienna – 1994 London). Ludwig Wittgenstein taught at the University of Cambridge from 1929 to 1947, until the 1930s his family in Vienna was at the center of cultural life, and his „Tractatus", first published in 1921 as „Logisch-Philosophische Abhandlung"[7], was one of the most influential publication in history of philosophy.[8] Karl Popper, one of the most famous philosophers in the 20th century who was knighted by Queen Elizabeth II in 1965, studied at the University of Vienna and received his doctoral degree in psychology in 1928 under the supervision of Karl Bühler. From 1929 to 1934 he was working as a schoolteacher in mathematics and physics, but continued to work scientifically. In 1934

---

[7] See Wittgenstein, Ludwig. Logisch-Philosophische Abhandlung. In: Annalen der Naturphilosophie, 14 (1921). In 1922 the english translation by C. K. Ogden was published under the title „Tractatus Logico-Philosophicus" (TLP).

[8] On L. Wittgenstein see Klagge, James Carl Wittgenstein: Biography and Philosophy. Cambridge: Cambridge University Press, 2001; Michael Nedo and Michele Ranchetti (eds.). Ludwig Wittgenstein: sein Leben in Bildern und Texten. Frankfurt/M.: Suhrkamp, 1983.

he published his book „Logik der Forschung" (The Logic of Scientific Discovery) where he developed his theory of potential falsifiability as the criterion to demark science from non-science. Looking for an academic position in UK in 1935/1936 he finally found a position as a lecturer in philosophy at Canterbury University College of the University of New Zealand in Christchurch in 1937. Here he wrote his influential book „The Open Society and its Enemies", published in 1945 in London in two volumes. In 1946 he became a reader in logic and scientific method at the London School of Economics, and from 1949 to 1969 he was professor of logic and scientific method at the University of London.

Because of the limited space of the paper it is impossible to write short sections about each member, about their relations as PhD students of M. Schlick or H. Hahn, for example, about their research topics and their contribution to the fields of philosophy and logic of science, history of science, sociology of science, and science studies. Some of them contributed to the development of physics like Ph. Frank, to mathematics like K. Gödel, R. von Mises, A. Tarski and Olga Taussky-Todd, to economics like O. Morgenstern and O. Neurath, to psychology like Karl and Charlotte Bühler. Some members were very active in the „Vienna Circle", preparing the international conferences, or Rudolf Carnap and Hans Reichenbach as editors of the journal from 1930 to 1939. Thanks to Rose Rand the records of discussions in the circle in the late 1920s and 1930s are kept.[9] She studied from 1924 to 1928 at the Vienna University with H. Gompertz, M. Schlick and R. Carnap, from 1930 to 1935 she was one of the most active participants. Only in 1938 she received her doctoral degree and had to go into exile immediately afterwards. She escaped to London but lived under difficult circumstances. In 1954 she moved to the USA where she was teaching philosophy at different universities.

---

[9] The records are kept in the Archive of the University Pittsburgh.

Like Ludwig Wittgenstein and Karl Popper, Rudolf Carnap, Hans Reichenbach and Rose Rand, most of the members of the „Vienna Circle", of the inner circle as well as of the periphery, had to go into exile because of the Nazi persecution. Some of them were Jewish and left-wings, therefore they tried to escape from Vienna from 1934 onwords. Like Karl Popper they often had to emigrate more than one time and to different countries. Otto Neurath – one of the leading figures of the „Vienna Circle" – first emigrated to The Netherlands where his wife Olga Hahn-Neurath died in 1937. After the beginning of WWII he and his later wife Marie Reidemeister fled to England, crossing the Channel with other refugees in an open boat. In Oxford he found a place where he could continue his work on the isotype system. Otto Neurath was not only a political economist but also a philosopher, a philosopher of science and a sociologist, he was working as a teacher and as a director of the museum, he was using statistics and studied languages to develop his system of isotypes.[10] Thanks to Marie Neurath and Robert S. Cohen (1923-2017), an American philosopher and historian of philosophy and science who edited the Boston Studies in Philosophy of Science for many decades, some work of O. Neurath was published posthumously. In 1973 they published „Empiricism and Sociology", and in 1983 they edited his „Philosophical Papers".[11]

All in all, 29 of 36 representatives of the „Vienna Circle" had to go into exile. The couple in science Olga Hahn-Neurath and Otto Neurath emigrated to The Netherlands, and in 1939 they had to go into exile

---

[10] See the excellent biography: Sandner, Günther. Otto Neurath. Eine politische Biographie. Vienna: Szolnay Publ., 2014.

[11] See Neurath, Marie and Cohen, Robert S. (eds) Empiricism and Sociology; The life and work of Otto Neurath. Dordrecht/Holland, Boston/USA: Reidel Publ., 1973; Neurath, Marie and Cohen, Robert S. (eds) Philosophical Papers. Dordrecht/Holland, Boston/USA. Reidel Publ., 1983. Furthermore, see Kraeutler, Hadwig. Otto Neurath. Museum and Exhibition Work – Spaces (Designed) for Communication. Frankfurt/M. et al: Peter Lang Verlag, 2008.

again. Only one (Josef Schächter) emigrated to Palestine, and Josef Frank (the architect) emigrated to Sweden. Whereas only five members finally escaped to UK, all in all 21 members emigrated to the USA. Therefore, the USA became the new homeland of analytical philosophy as well as of post- and neo-positivism, and of logical positivism. Here philosophy and logic of science, history of science, sociology of science, and science studies were further developed, partly by the emigrées and later by their students and followers. Only very rarely were the emigrées asked to offer lectures in their former home country, and only very late were they remembered at the University of Vienna, and at University of Berlin.

At Berlin University a small group was working. First of all, from 1920 to 1933 the mathematician and aerodynamicist Richard von Mises (1883-1953) was full professor and director of the newly established Institute for Applied Mathematics at the Berlin University. In 1926 Hans Reichenbach (1891-1953) became an assistant professor (ausserordentlicher Professor) of philosophy of physics at the Berlin University. He studied mathematics, physics and philosophy, in 1915 he received the doctoral degree at the University of Erlangen. His thesis „Der Begriff der Wahrscheinlichkeit für die mathematische Darstellung der Wirklichkeit" (On the notion of probability as mathematical description of the reality) was written under the supervisors Max Noether (1844-1921) – the father of the mathematicians Emmy Noether (1882-1935) and Fritz Noether (1884-1941) – and Paul Hensel (1860-1930) – a relative (great-grandson) of Moses Mendelssohn (1729-1786).[12] In the winter 1917/18 he worked

---

[12] See Vogt, Annette. Moses Mendelssohn and his family – Haskalah and mathematics. In: Bergmann, Birgit, Epple, Moritz, Unger, Ruti (eds) Transcending Tradition. Jewish Mathematicians in German-Speaking Academic Culture. Heidelberg et al: Springer, 2012, pp. 45-50. On Emmy Noether see Rowe, David. On Stage and Behind the Scenes in Göttingen: Otto Blumenthal, Richard Courant, Emmy Noether and Paul Bernays.

together with Albert Einstein (1879-1955) in Berlin, and thanks to the support of A. Einstein became an assistant professor in 1926. From 1930 to 1931 Gustav Bergmann (1906-1987) came as a PhD student from Vienna to Berlin to study with H. Reichenbach. From 1930 to 1939 Hans Reichenbach and Rudolf Carnap were the editors of the journal „Erkenntnis" (knowledge) which became the journal of the „Vienna Circle".

The Vienna Circle – the scientific disciplines

Regarding the scientific disciplines of the representatives of the „Vienna Circle", we'll give only an overview and mention here the figures and names of representatives:

14 philosophers – M. Schlick, R. Carnap, H. Feigl, B. Juhos, V. Kraft, Rose Rand (she kept records of the discussions), E. Zilsel as members of the inner circle, and H. Gomperz, C. G. Hempel, E. S. Kaila, A. Naess, E. Nagel, and to add L. Wittgenstein and K. Popper;

10 mathematicians – G. Bergmann, K. Gödel, H. Hahn, Olga Hahn-Neurath, K. Menger, R. v. Mises, Fr. Waisman(n) as members of the inner circle, and K. Reidemeister, A. Tarski, and Olga Taussky-Todd.

There were only two physicists – Philipp Frank and Hans Reichenbach –, and two economists – beside Otto Neurath Oskar Morgenstern participated in some discussions, two lawyers – F. Kaufmann and H. Kelsen, and the later Rabbi Josef Schächter. Additionally 4 psychologists belonged to the circles, these were the

---

In: Bergmann, Birgit, Epple, Moritz, Unger, Ruti (eds) Transcending Tradition. Jewish Mathematicians in German-Speaking Academic Culture. Heidelberg et al. Springer, 2012, pp. 79-87.

2 couples in sciences Egon Brunswik and Else Frenkel-Brunswik and Karl Bühler and Charlotte Bühler.[13] Josef Frank, the brother of Philipp Frank, was the only architect who participated in the circles. Among the four promoters Frank P. Ramsey was a mathematician and economist, the three others were philosophers.

The Vienna Circle – the scientific activities

The scientific activities of the members of the „Vienna Circle" became more visible when they organised international conferences, called „Kongress für wissenschaftliche Philosophie" (congress for scientific philosophy). All in all eight such congresses took place, beginning in 1929. The next congress was held already a year later in 1930 in Königsberg (at that time in Germany, today Kaliningrad (Russia)). Because of the political situation in Austria in 1934 the next congress took place in 1934 in Prague. Although the political situation in Europe became complicated because of the rise of Nazism, the organisers were able to hold congresses in 1935 in Paris and in 1936 in Copenhagen, the last one in Europe took place in 1938 in Cambrigde (UK). One year later the scholars moved to Cambridge (USA) where in 1939 the seventh congress was held, and the last one took place in 1941 in Chicago. Meanwhile the Nazi's had occupied most of Europe, many members of the „Vienna Circle" fled the persecution, and there was no time and spirit anymore for conferences and congresses like this. The scientists among the refugees, the physicists and mathematicians, took part in

---

[13] On the concept of couples in sciences see Pycior, Helena M., Slack, Nancy G. and Abir-Am, Pnina G. (eds.), Creative Couples in the Sciences, New Brunswick/New Jersey: Rutgers University Press 1996.

war activities to participate in WW II against the Nazi's.

After the first congress, in 1929, the „Manifesto" of the „Vienna Circle" was published. The main author was Otto Neurath, and he was also the initiator of this kind of publication. In the „Manifesto" was argued the „world conception" (Weltauffassung) of the authors, the aim of their meetings and discussions. Here they announced: „We witness the spirit of the scientific world conception penetrating in growing measure the forms of personal and public life, in education, upbringing, architecture, and the shaping of economic and social life according to rational principles. The scientific world conception serves life and life receives it."[14]

The „Manifesto" listed several names of people who never participated, and mentioned Albert Einstein, Bertrand Russell and Ludwig Wittgenstein as its „leading representatives" – thus, the myth of the circle began. In detail, the „Manifesto" listed Walter Dubislav, Josef Frank, Kurt Grelling, Hasso Härlen, Eino Kaila, Heinrich Loewy, F. P. Ramsey, Hans Reichenbach, Kurt Reidemeister, and Edgar Zilsel as people „sympathetic to the Vienna Circle" and Albert Einstein, Bertrand Russell, and Ludwig Wittgenstein as its „leading representatives". When one compare this list of names with the reconstructed list of members of the „Vienna Circle" above, one see that the myth of the circle began just here.

Independently from this activity, and the partly idealistic positions as announced in the „Manifesto", the contributions of the members of the „Vienna Circle" were remarkable. The most important output of their activities were the journal and several books, published over a long period. From 1930 to 1939/1940 Rudolf Carnap (1891-1970) and Hans Reichenbach (1891-1953) edited the journal „Erkenntnis"

---

[14] See Manifesto, 1929, for further explanations see Sandner, Günther. Otto Neurath. Eine politische Biographie. Vienna: Szolnay Publ., 2014.

as an international Journal for Analytical Philosophy. The journal was published from 1919 until 1929 under the title „Annalen der Philosophie". When R. Carnap and H. Reichenbach became the new editors, the journal was supported by the Society of empirical philosophy Berlin and the Ernst Mach Society Vienna (Gesellschaft fur empirische Philosophie, Berlin and Vereins Ernst Mach, Wien). After the beginning of WW II in 1939 the journal was re-named as „Journal of unified science (Erkenntnis) „, edited by O. Neurath, R. Carnap, and Charles Morris from the University of Chicago, and it was published now in University Chicago Press. Unfortunately, the journal lasted only one year, from 1939 to 1940. The new title underlined still the project – or the dream – of a unified science, and it was the optimism of O. Neurath and Charles Morris to believe that the journal will have a future on the American continent after the beginning of WW II. Only in 1975 the journal was re-founded and edited by Wilhelm K. Essler, Carl G. Hempel (1905-1997), and Wolfgang Stegmüller (1923-1991). It still exists, and the editor in 2017 is Hannes Leitgeb (b.1972), professor at the (LMU) University of Munich.

Another important result of the „Vienna Circle" are the books, published from 1928 onwards by members of the circle. There were three book series, the first was published between 1928 and 1937 under the general title „Schriften zur wissenschaftlichen Weltauffassung" (Monographs on the Scientific World-Conception), edited by M. Schlick and Ph. Frank. The second series „Einheitswissenschaft" (Unified Science) was started in 1933 and edited by Otto Neurath, the volumes were published in The Hague (The Netherlands) where he was living in exile. In this series under the title „Library of unified science" the book of Richard von Mises „Positivism. A Study in human understanding" was published in 1939 as Volume I. Later the series became the IEUS: The International Encyclopedia of Unified Science, edited by O. Neurath († 1945), R. Carnap († 1970) and Charles W. Morris († 1979). The IEUS came out in Chicago between 1938 and 1970, it was never finished. Only the first section, „Foundations of the Unity of Science" (FUS), of the IEUS was published, it contains two volumes with a total of 20 monographs, published from 1938 to 1970. The IEUS was the last book project and became partly the legacy of the „Vienna Circle".

To give the reader an impression of the importance of this series and to mention the authors who belonged for shorter or longer time to the „Vienna Circle" or later joined this project, the book titles and the authors are listed here:

Vol. I, Numbers 1-10
Encyclopedia and Unified Science (FUS I-1) – Otto Neurath et al[15]
Foundations of the Theory of Signs (FUS I-2) – Charles W. Morris
Foundations of Logic and Mathematics (FUS I-3) – Rudolf Carnap
Linguistic Aspects of Science (FUS I-4) – Leonard Bloomfield
Procedures of Empirical Sciences (FUS I-5) – Victor Lenzen
Principles of the Theory of Probability (FUS I-6) – (1939) – Ernest
    Nagel
Foundations of Physics (FUS I-7) – Philipp Frank
Cosmology (FUS I-8) – E. Finlay-Freundlich
Foundations of Biology (FUS I-9) – Felix Mainx
The Conceptual Framework of Psychology (FUS I-10) – Egon
    Brunswik
Vol. II, Numbers 1-10
Foundations of the Social Sciences (FUS II-1) – Otto Neurath
The Structure of Scientific Revolutions (FUS II-2) – Thomas S.

---

[15] The authors were beside Otto Neurath, Niels Bohr, John Dewey, Bertrand Russell, Rudolf Carnap, and Charles Morris.

Kuhn

Science and the Structure of Ethics (FUS II-3) – Abraham Edel

Theory of Valuation (FUS II-4) – John Dewey

The Technique of Theory Construction (FUS II-5) – Joseph Henry Woodger

Methodology of Mathematical Economics and Econometrics (FUS II-6) – Gerhard Tintner

Fundamentals of Concept Formation in Empirical Science (FUS II-7) – Carl G. Hempel

The Development of Rationalism and Empiricism (FUS II-8) – George De Santillana, Edgar Zilsel

The Development of Logical Empiricism (FUS II-9) – Joergen Joergensen

Bibliography and Index (FUS II-10) – Herbert Feigl, Charles Morris

Charles W. (William) Morris (1901-1979), the US semiotician and philosopher who travelled in 1934 through Europe and met B. Russell and in Vienna R. Carnap, O. Neurath, and M. Schlick, was impressed by logical positivism. He became the most vocal advocate in the United States for Otto Neurath's „Unity of Science Movement". During the 1930s, Morris helped several German and Austrian philosophers to emigrate to the United States, including Rudolf Carnap in 1936. As a part of the „Unity of Science Movement", Morris worked together closely with Neurath and Carnap on the project of the „International Encyclopedia of Unified Science" (IEUS) until 1943, and again after 1945 until the early 1970s.

Among the authors of Vol. II we mention especially Thomas S. Kuhn (1922-1996) who published his „The Structure of Scientific Revolutions" in 1962 in Chicago (the German edition came out in 1967). He was a physicist and a historian and philosopher of science.

In 1949 he received his PhD in physics at Harvard University, later he investigated the history of physics. The HSS (History of Science Society) awarded him the Sarton Medal in 1982. Kuhn's book played an important role in the history of science, it was translated into several languages and was re-published several times.[16]

The author of the book „Methodology of Mathematical Economics and Econometrics" (FUS II-6) Gerhard Tintner (1907 Nuremberg – 1983 Vienna) studied economy at the University of Vienna, and in 1929 he recieved his PhD under the supervisor Ludwig von Mises (1881-1973), the elder brother of Richard von Mises. In 1936 he emigrated to the USA, in 1973 he moved back to Vienna.

The brothers Ludwig and Richard von Mises were quite different, not only related to their scientific disciplines – economy versus mathematics –, but also related to their attitude to the „Vienna Circle". In contrast to Ludwig von Mises his brother Richard von Mises partcipated in discussions in this circle, and during his exile in Turkey[17] he was working for the project on unified science.

The Vienna Circle – the scientific legacy

The scientific legacy of the „Vienna Circle" is the publications of their members, especially the publications in the journal „Erkenntnis" (1930-1939), and the many books in the three series, mentioned above. These publications are the scientific outcome of the „Vienna Circle"

---

[16] On the 50th anniversary of his book many colloquia took place, and articles and books about him and his book were published. See Richards, Robert J., Daston, Lorraine (eds) Kuhn's Structure of Scientific Revolutions at Fifty. Reflections on a Science Classic. Chicago: University of Chicago Press, 2016.

[17] On the exile in Turkey see Reisman, Arnold. Turkey's Modernization. Refugees from Nazism and Atatürk's Vision. Washington D.C.: New Academia Publishing, 2006.

and its members as well as the legacy. These books should be re-read, should be studied under the new circumstances in the 21st century, should be discussed from the today's perspective. This is true not only for the book of Thomas S. Kuhn which influenced the development of the history of science for more than 50 years. Similar investigations could be done for other books in these series.

As an example, we will underline the fate, the circumstances, and the aims of the publication of Richard von Mises (1883-1953), his book „Positivism. A Study in human understanding". As already mentioned, it was published as Volume I of the series „Library of unified science, book series". The manuscript was written (in German) in exile in Istanbul, the book came out in German (Kleines Lehrbuch des Positivismus) in a publishing house in The Hague in 1939, shortly before the beginning of WW II. The foreword was dated January 1939. An english translation of this book was published only in 1951, and only in 1990 it was re-published in German.[18] R. v. Mises remembered in the preface to the english version Ernst Mach and Henri Poincaré, the „Vienna Circle" and especially Otto Neurath, whom he described as „an unusually clear thinker, a polyhistor [meaning? poly historian?], a successful writer and brilliant speaker, and he had a unique goal in life: the improvement of human understanding."[19]

The editors of the series „Library of unified science, book series"

---

[18] See in detail: von Mises, Richard. Kleines Lehrbuch des Positivismus. Einführung in die empiristische Wissenschaftsauffassung. The Hague, Holland: W. P. van Stockum & Zoon, 1939 (467 pp.). The series title was: Library of unified science, book series. And the editors were: Otto Neurath Editor-in-chief; Rudolf Carnap, Philipp Frank, Jorgen Jorgensen, Charles W. Morris. – von Mises, Richard. Positivism. A study in human understanding. Cambridge: Harvard Univ. Press, 1951 (404 pp.); translated by Jerry Bernstein and Roger G. Newton. Copyright by the President and Fellows of Harvard College. – von Mises, Richard. Positivismus. Einführung in die empiristische Wissenschaftsauffassung. Edited and introduced by Friedrich Stadler. Frankfurt/M.: Suhrkamp Verlag, suhrkamp taschenbuch wissenschaft, 1990 (559 pp.).

[19] See von Mises (1951), p. VI (preface, dated August 1950).

in which the book of R. von Mises came out as Volume I in 1939 – Otto Neurath (1882-1945), Rudolf Carnap (1891-1970), Philipp Frank (1884-1964), and Charles W. Morris (1901-1979) – contributed to the development of positivism and to the ideal of a „unified science" at different times. The book series „Library of unified science" was an output of the „Vienna Circle" as well as a development of its own, regarding the circumstances after the abrupt end of the circle in the 1930s, the displacement of many scholars who were involved in the discussions, and their escape into exile. And it was an unfinished project with many influences on new scientific disciplines like philosophy and logic of science, history of science, sociology of science, and science studies.

Conclusion

When in 1929 the „The Manifesto" of the „Vienna Circle" was declared, an initiative of Otto Neurath, and the ideal of the „unified science" was announced, the group of the different scholars became well-known. From this year several international conferences were organised, the journal was edited from 1930 on, and the book series „Library of unified science" was planned. Because of the political and economical circumstances, first the great depression, then the Nazi's in Germany and later in Austria, volume I of this series came out only in 1939, shortly before WW II. As we have seen, the „Vienna Circle" wasn't only one circle, it had a kind of sub-circles, and a small group of its representatives was working in Berlin, especially the philosopher Hans Reichenbach and the mathematician and aerodynamicist Richard von Mises who published the book „Positivism. A Study in human understanding" in 1939 as volume I in the series.

The book series „Library of unified science" was an output of the „Vienna Circle" as well as a development of its own, regarding the circumstances after the abrupt end of the circle in the 1930s, the displacement of many scholars who were involved in the discussions, and their escape into exile. And it was an unfinished project with many influences on new scientific disciplines like philosophy and logic of science, history of science, sociology of science, and science studies. The editors of the series „Library of unified science, book series" Otto Neurath, Rudolf Carnap, Philipp Frank, and Charles W. Morris contributed to the development of positivism and to the ideal of the „unified science" at different times.

The „Vienna Circle", i. e. the place in Vienna and the way how philosophers and physicists, mathematicians, economists and sociologists discussed together and against each other, became most famous in the period between 1918 and 1934/36. These debates and their outcomes – the publications, the journal and the book series – played an important role in history of philosophy as well as in history of science. Whereas the ideal of the „unified science" is still an open research question, the development of philosophy, sociology, and history of science was deeply influenced by the thinkers who belonged to the „Vienna Circle" in its inner circle or arround it. Thomas Kuhn's famous book „The structure of scientific revolution", published in the series „Library of unified science, book series" in 1962 became a key publication in history of science, the celebration of its publication in 2016 made clear how deeply this book has influenced the development of modern history of science. On the other side, Kuhn's book was a late echo of those discussions between philosophers and physicists in Vienna. Historians of science today are linked with this inheritance in one way or another.

Letters Matters, Mathematics and Bibliotherapy

Existential intensity, that is all what we are looking for

Florentin Bosse

The interdisciplinary theory[1] is the very proof that the categorisation thinking, the alleged "inner desire" to put things that we see or think into boxes has a limited value and it emphasises in the mean time the fluidity of space, time and reality (which are questionable entities in themselves)…The glue that brings the different elements of our rationale called "disciplines" – among which humanities, social sciences and science – together is the intensity of the each of our undertakings and its variations of intensity.

Literature, bibliotherapy and mathematics – categories, of course, which I want to talk about – converge in enriching one's life. By considering possible definitions of what a novel or a mathematical structure is, it is argued that the fundamental difference between conventional mathematics and artistic literature is one of form rather than content and bibliotherapy – better said self-bibliotherapy – is the magic wand that shapes both mathematics and artistic literature in a subliminal, intense journey. But apart from arguing the above, the very living proof of applied interdisciplinary theory is in front of your eyes.

1.1 Ideas and principles – Definitions

Why should we talk about math in an essay about literature or why should we talk about literature in a mathematical paper? I have two

---

[1] Rick Szostak – Defining interdisciplinarity
https://sites.google.com/a/ualberta.ca/rick-szostak/research/about-interdisciplinarity/definitions/defining-instrumental-interdisciplinarity

distinct reasons for this. In the first place, because ultimately, the value of literature and mathematics is that they both attempt to give a meaning to our life through their intensity. Life itself seems meaningless but it acquires value to us because we, somehow, have created ways to enjoy our individual and collective existences. I can't see any reason to doubt that art, scientific knowledge and thinking itself are noble ways to sense and intensify one's life. In fact, until the 18th and 19th centuries, universities traditionally considered mathematics as part of the humanities, especially as a branch of philosophical thought; on how the mind operates in arriving at conclusions, on how we connect what we think to the world as it appears to us. So mathematics was a way to connect mind and world.

Therefore, "the persistence of the rhetoric of "two cultures," one scientific, the other humanities-based, obscures the porous border and productive relationship that has long existed between literature and mathematics"[2]. In fact, in eighteenth-century Scottish universities, geometry in particular was considered one of the humanities; anchored in philosophy, it instilled what we call critical thinking

1.1.1 Literature

The definition of Literature has changed over centuries several times, so that possibly a historicist approach to understand that Literature might be most appropriate. In any case, the only certain thing about defining Literature is that the very definition of it will change over time again. But what we do know about it and its effects is that Literature

---

[2] Rick Szostak – Defining interdisciplinarity
  https://sites.google.com/a/ualberta.ca/rick-szostak/research/about-interdisciplinarity/
  definitions/defining-instrumental-interdisciplinarity

and reading makes us nicer people, it makes us discover, create and understand ourselves, it is helping developing the verbal activities, improves our focus, concentration and memory and improves the ways of expressing ourselves in a more elaborate and imaginative way.

1.1.2 Mathematics

Mathematics is a language, in that it allows us to express ideas and notions that are hard or impossible to communicate otherwise. Music or literature is a language in precisely this sense, too. For more than two thousand years, mathematics has been a part of the human search for understanding. Mathematical discoveries have come both from the attempt to describe the natural world and from the desire to arrive at a form of irrevocable truth from careful and logical reasoning.

> *Mathematics is generally categorized as a science, but I do believe that it is more than that. Arguably, mathematical discoveries are made regardless of their applicability or utility to the physical world. Mathematics has evolved purely for itself, with the greatest contributions to the field being those theories that put value on the beauty of the adopted logic. The mystery of mathematics is that, as any great theory, has an inherent, embedded beauty that transcends the subject in a subliminal way and sometimes finds applicability in other fields. But that is just the mystery.*

1.1.3 Bibliotherapy

Life's too short for bad books – but where too start? Millions of books are published every year; blogs, tweets, posts and homepages are overpopulating the clouds …

In the 13th century Before Christ there was a phrase written above the entrance to the royal chamber library where books were stored by King Ramses II of Egypt, – considered to be the oldest known library motto in the world – which reads: "This is the house of healing for the soul"[3] … we should let this sentence flow and taste over our palate for a little while…

In its most basic form, bibliotherapy involves the systematic use of books to help people cope with the issues that they may be facing at a particular time (physical, emotional, developmental, mental or social problems). It consists of selecting reading material relevant to a person's life situation. Bibliotherapy has also been explained – in a nutshell – as being "a process of dynamic interaction between the personality of the reader and literature-interaction which may be utilized for personal assessment, adjustment, and growth"[4].

In an extended sense, though, the impulse we have sometimes of just entering into a bookshop, search a book, review a few pages, have a coffee, and feel somehow transcended in another world is nothing else but what I would call unconscious self-induced bibliotherapy.

1.1.4 *Intensity*

Intensity is the measure of what can not be measured, is the quantity of what can not be quantified and the value of what can not be assessed.

Actually intensity, in a non-elaborated way, is nothing other than the principle of systematically comparing a thing to itself. Intense is what is more or less strongly what it is.

---

[3] Matthew Wickman. *Literature after Euclid,* Haney foundation.
[4] Lehr, Fran. (1981). Bibliotherapy. *Journal of Reading,* 25.

"Something may be disgusting, terrible, provocative, ambitious, exciting, melancholic, depressing, bold, poignant, repulsive, criminal… Nothing can be a priori excluded. What it is, does not count. The important thing is, to be at its greatest and at its best. Even the weakness can still be loved, praised and celebrated, if it is in a strong way manifested weakness. Intensity is everything. One can be in a mediocre way bright. Better, if one had been splendidly mediocre"[5].

We can only feel what is intense, that is, what increases, decreases, changes. That is why we can not quantify the intensity, as it can not be quantified what one feels. Perhaps this is what defines us. Serenity, excitement, joy, fear, sadness, belief and enlightment… all forms of intensity of "something" we can not articulate, but feel – and in a way, are maybe consciously or unconsciously longing for.

There is latent and erupting intensity in both mathematics and literature; in art or science, in love or hate. And it is this intensity that captivates us and instinctively and in a sophisticated way makes us addicted to whatever we do. It is the fountain that contains the living ever after water we are all searching for.

1.2 Examples to reflect on the ideas and principles

1.2.1 Letters Matters

It all started October 2015, when I returned from my six months self exile from society – or, "retreat", the word people use nowadays for the time one needs to question the unquestionable questions – undertaking a solitary pilgrimage from Berlin to Santiago de Compostella and then

---

[5] Tristan Garcia. *The intensive Life.*

further to Portugal; a pilgrimage which brought me back trust, nature, wisdom and love. I started that pilgrimage after working 30 years in technology, using mathematics, logical thinking and questioning, rationale and abstraction. I came back from that pilgrimage with a clear sense of purpose and a mission.

Perhaps all started a long time ago, though, when I was Robinson Crusoe, D'Artagnan, Holden Caulfield, Oliver Twist, Prince Myshkin, and many others…while exceling in math, physics and chemistry at school, as science matters were by large as the best socially accepted recipe for a successful, reliable and rewarding professional life.

I came back from my pilgrimage with this strong feeling that nowadays seems to be a painful search all the way through our community for regaining authenticity, authenticity of our values and our purpose. We are in a way lost in this technocratic society, have this perception of uneasiness that can not be articulated and try to find social niches for breathing empathy and surviving our social and possibly derived personal unhappiness. We seem to not be able to defend ourselves any more and we can not hide ourselves from the outside world where multitasking and switching focus every five seconds from one social media to another seems to be the mother of all things.

So I came up with this idea to trying to promote bibliotherapy, give people back the reading. Needless to say, you can not give people back the reading as a birthday or Christmas present. So the challenge was and is mountain high. I embarked on this journey of creating a special retreat, a space of harmony, wisdom and emotional well being called "Letters Matters"; a bookshop that exhibits the best books ever written. A bookshop that lives through the breathing of over 500 curators, who gave me the book titles of the best 10 books they have ever read. You can read a book here in the bookshop, drink a coffee, play a game of chess, a game of Go or explore any other mental, memory or thinking challenges, have a unique culinary experience, drink a glass of wine and have a good conversation (literary, or maybe philosophical, existential or social-political) with a friend or one of our curators. It is an atmosphere bookshop, an emotional bookshop, a bibliotherapy atelier, an inspiration and a motivation bookshop, as well as a workshop for teaching, learning and feeling the intensity of having a good time.

The intensity of life, the joy and fulfilment I felt throughout this project and beyond enriched my life experience with such a power and perplexity, like a waterfall which you hear but not see and out of a sudden, getting out of the forest, you become speechless, completely sensorial paralysed and realize where that breaking noise was coming from... The perception of the unique Nothingness I am in this cosmic, maybe metaphysical world we inherited and bear our Nothingness in, together with the feeling of my authenticity of Being; and yet being able to communicate – sometimes even beyond words or formulae – with other Nothingness, made me feel sacred and religious in a way, as it humbled me and empowered me in the same time.

And yes, that place was bringing all the puzzle pieces together, mathematics, literature, philosophy and philology, contradiction and mistrust, dreams and life intensity, bibliotherapy and art... science and humanities ...

1.2.2 Literature and Mathematics

There is a long history of seeing the irrational, the intuitive, as being the essence of scientific or artistic genius, often viewed as a kind of contact with divine forces, even verging on madness: the poet, the philosopher or the mathematician as the chosen one. Immanuel Kant defined genius as "the innate mental predisposition (ingenium) through which nature gives the rule to art"[5]. In other words, genius is the way in which some people can directly apprehend truths about nature, without the need for logical deduction.

In this way of thinking, logic can take us only so far; genius then has to take over. Using a sequence of logical steps it's possible to produce a piece of work that is beautiful, but genius can carry us beyond beauty. This state beyond beauty is an immeasurable and ephemeral state – called "the sublime", or maybe divine.

According to Edmund Burke, "beauty is what gives us pleasure, but the sublime is associated with fear. Well-tended gardens, properly proportioned buildings – these are beautiful. A storm at sea, wild mountains, the infinity of space, the thought of death – these are sublime"[56]. Artists and scientists of the Romantic period became preoccupied with these sublime themes, and they themselves were increasingly seen as heroic figures, delving into areas of experience unavailable to lesser mortals. This was the image of Byron, Beethoven or Einstein, people with wild hair, furiously and with full-throttle intensity, scribbling away at divinely inspired work penetrating the deepest mysteries of the universe.

Differences

When we compare mathematics and literature we can immediately think of differences. Mathematics is typically seen as abstract, remote from everyday experiences and emotions, whereby literature seems to be quite the opposite. Mathematics is logical and analytic – literature is intuitive and expressive.

---

[6] Jorge Alejandro Laris Pardo. „Infinities in literature and mathematics".

To most people, the difference is apparent simply by comparing the appearance of a mathematical text with a literary one. There is a language of mathematics with its symbols and terminology, mysterious to non-specialists, while most literary works are written in a language, which, if not always of the "everyday" kind, is at least familiar. In artistic texts such as novels and poetry, we find that particular words a writer uses are of great importance to the aesthetic effect; it is often remarked that poetry, in particular loses something in translation. With mathematics, the situation is quite different – we could even say that mathematics is concerned precisely with those things that are invariant under linguistic translation, so in other words an universal language, perhaps. In that sense, there is not really a "language" of mathematics; rather, mathematics is an abstraction of whatever can be said equally in any natural language.

But maybe we should try to examine more closely the notion that mathematics is purely logical while literature is intuitive. Mathematicians themselves have long taken issue with this – mathematics can also be intuitive, as Henri Poincaré emphasized.

He maintained that great mathematicians could be of either intuitionalists or logicians, but he made a special plea for intuition, saying that rigor alone could not suffice. "In becoming rigorous, mathematical science takes a character so artificial as to strike every one; it forgets its historical origins; we see how the questions can be answered, we no longer see how and why they are put. This shows us that logic is not enough; that the science of demonstration is not all science and that intuition must retain its role as complement, if you want, as counterpart or as antidote of logic"[7]. So among mathematicians there has always been a sense of needing to strike a

---

[7] Emmer M, Quarteroni Mathknow, Vol 3 – Springer Verlag Italia 2009.

balance between intuition and logic; and because outsiders tend to see only the logical side of mathematics, mathematicians themselves are quite keen to highlight the intuitive aspect.

If we talk purely about mathematics, according to an often-repeated remark attributed to Gauss, mathematics is the "queen of sciences"; and when D'Alembert classified scientific knowledge in the Encyclopedia, he placed mathematics at the foundation. He said that "the claim of theoretical physics to be the most "fundamental" science rests on its being the most mathematical, the most abstract, the most remote from everyday experience" – as far as possible, in fact, from what we might consider the normal domain of artistic literature!!

On the other hand, it is maybe relevant to mention Alain Badiou's courageous statement, when he stated: "math is ontology itself". But, as Badiou — and Plato well before him — has stated, "Even when math offers true knowledge, it alone cannot suffice for wisdom. For mathematical knowledge to turn into wisdom it is necessary to include philosophy, and literature"[8].

Similarities

On a practical level of analysis, though, when we look at mathematics and literature as human activities, there are obvious similarities. Writers, like mathematicians, spend a lot of time sitting at their desk, trying to come up with a good idea. They get annoyed and wrestle with problems existing only in the mind, have moments of inspiration, try to work out the implications that follow, and find yet more ideas.

---

[8] https://www.bu.edu/wcp/Papers/Aest/AestGilm.htm

Both disciplines have a common mass of "classic" works, which we can go and find in any library.

There is a deeper and more philosophical connection, and it concerns the very existence of those objects that the writer or mathematician deals with: the ontology connection.

In literature, for example, Hamlet – in Shakespeare's play – sees the ghost of his father, and one can ask: is the ghost real? One answer is yes: the play is set in a world where ghosts exist. Another is no: the play is set in our world, and the ghost is an illusion. Another is that there is no ghost, and no Hamlet – none of the characters is real.

But then, in mathematics, what about those other characters who inhabit mathematics, the irrational or imaginary numbers, say? Are they a real thing, or a pure mathematical imagination as metaphysical or even ontological explanation for mathematically unexplainable things?

How surreal can be a valid mathematical equation like e ** iπ +1 = 0 , which brings together elements, symbols discovered by different scientists in different times and places?

("e" – discovered by Leonhard Euler, Suisse 18th century, "i" – discovered by Heron of Alexandria, Egypt 1st century, "π" – discovered by Archimedes, Greece 4th century BC and Boolean algebra – discovered by George Boole, England, 19th century). You feel such an intense and deep belonging to history, humanity and maybe even religion, as one might consider that it can only be "God's hand" to reveal the intense, sublime beauty of that equation.

As far as divinity is concerned, such a mathematical sublime beauty – which can be demonstrated, of course, and I am happy to perform this demonstration if needed – stays strong compared with any other famous pieces of work, like Marquez's "One hundred years of solitude" or Hesse's "The glass bead game".

Joining the dots

At the beginning of the 20th century, alongside this desire for more formalism in mathematics, there was also a school of formalism in the theory of the novel.

The formalist view was that language has structure, and that literature has analogous structures at a higher level. The formalists were interested in the beginning in narrative structure, not the particular way in which narrative is presented, but later, toward the end of the 20th century they looked specifically at language, isolating its "functions" and classifying them according to how they are oriented (for example towards a listener, towards oneself, towards establishing contact, etc.) This way of thinking influenced people in other disciplines, in particular the anthropologist Claude Lévi-Strauss, who, with a lot of enthusiasm, energy and intensity looked for structures in the culture of Amazonian tribes-people and developed his theories. He was considered the founder of Structuralism, which took the idea of linguistic structure and applied it to culture in general. So, if we follow the logical stream and the historical perspective, formalism (in the sense of identifying and developing structure) in mathematics generated formalism in literature, which subsequently generated formalism in language, which in turn made Structuralism emerge in culture…

How is that for a cross-boundary evolution of thinking, where categories like sc*ience, art, literature, anthropology, structuralism,* *communities and humanities are getting simply blasted away and a continuous penetration of desire of making knowledge wisdom, through intensity of our living experiences is taking over?*

Intertwining

Nowadays, in a time of tireless hunting for intense sensorial impressions and euphoria generating events, it seems that the masters of abstraction (mathematicians that is) become heroes of best-read books.

An answer to this is, first of all, that the object of the public fascination is not necessarily the thing in itself. But, of course, the artistic concept these days is precisely this: to create something and then create some other thing that gives people the impression that they have understood that first something. They would then intensely feel that they participate and have an experience that goes beyond the realm of the everyday.

And precisely because mathematics has the highest degree of abstraction from all sciences and is, in principle, most incomprehensible even for most mathematicians, it is excellently suited to the awe-inspiring mystery. Since almost no one understands mathematics, everything can be asserted of it, which makes mathematics an ideal postmodern communication theme.

"Could that be because historical fiction novels were understood as a disguise of math calculus? Or poems were enacting the formation and breakdown of community feelings as the history of expositions of irrational numbers? What if, in other words, literary texts possessed a kind of mathematical unconscious?"[9]

---

[9] https://english.stackexchange.com

We might not know and never find out why and how, but there is a definite transcendental attraction between mathematics and literature. And I would like to tell you a story about this magic, intertwining subliminal attraction – it is the Fermat theorem story.

Fermat's theorem

When the problem is finally solved at the beginning of the 21st century the answer runs to 100 pages of dense mathematical logic. The British mathematician, who solved the famous puzzle 20 years ago, is credited with creativity, generosity, intuition and heroism. So the narrative provides a thread that extends across 26 centuries, and winds through some enjoyable instruction for newcomers (and that's most of us) to number theory. This includes the separation of numbers into deficient, excessive and perfect 6 and 28 are perfect, for example, because they are the sum of their divisors (6 – 1, 2 and 3 and 28 – 1, 2, 4, 7 and 14) and the realization that numbers are hidden in everything, from the harmonics of a musical note to the orbits of the planets and the meanders of rivers.

It is also refreshing to discover that thanks to Pierre de Fermat we can be sure there is one and only one number in the infinite progression of all possible numbers that immediately follows a square and immediately precedes a cube. It is 26, a number distinguished hitherto only by being the number of letters in the Latin alphabet. All numbers seem more interesting, because of this beautiful book, even 26: how's that for an unexpected consequence?

It is difficult to say what one feels or realizes while contemplating about these things. It must be magic, genius or some sort of higher Force that comprehends and generates all things; we all try, knowingly

or not, with intensity and ardor to get a sense in all what we see and feel,
a sense for all things that we can not logically grasp and the intensity of
that feeling is rocketing while reading these books. It must be something
out there beyond logic or intuition or pure narrative depiction.

A final thought about the inexplicable and yet unavoidable unity of mathematics and literature

There is one last thing that I would like, to share with you, a thing that obsessed me from the early school years. I do not remember any longer which was the first discipline and which was the second one, when I learnt about parable, hyperbole, metaphor and ellipsis – math first and then in literature or the other way around. But for sure, I was really confused about the fact that we use the same words with such different meanings. I asked my math teacher ad he could not give me any explanation. I asked my literature teacher and she could not give me any explanation. I was quite frustrated, and the fact the metaphor did not have a geometrical figure, frustrated me even more.

I kept that secret with me for years, hoping one day to find an answer. And I eventually did. – Apart from the metaphor, but I left that for you to do the research on. So here we go:

Hyperbole, ellipsis, parabola – they are mathematical, geometrical figures, but also literary instruments for describing and comparing things

There are three geometric curves known as conic sections:

Ellipse: a curve on a plane surrounding two focal points such that a straight line drawn from one of the focal points to any point on the curve and then back to the other focal point has the same length for every point on the curve.

Parabola: a two-dimensional, mirror symmetrical curve, which is approximately U-shaped.

Hyperbola: has two pieces, called connected components or branches that are mirror images of each other and resemble two infinite bows.

There are also three terms in linguistics with analogous names (in many languages with the same names, actually):

Ellipsis: the omission from a clause of one or more words that are nevertheless understood in the context of the remaining elements.

Parable: a succinct, didactic story, in prose or verse, which illustrates one or more instructive lessons or principles.

Hyperbole: is the use of exaggeration as a rhetorical device or figure of speech.

Apparently there was no relation or similarity between the literary and mathematical notions, except for the onomastics – so I thought.

But then again:

"A *parabola* is a – using Latin-derived morphs an 'apposition' or 'adjacency'.

In rhetoric, it is a comparison, which sets two terms side-by-side; later it denotes a fiction, which is 'set beside' and **parallels** ('lies next to') reality

In geometry, it is a conic section formed by the intersection of a cone with a plane with ***the same*** inclination to the axis as one of the cone's sides – the plane is **parallel** to that side. (*as seen on the next page*)

A *hyperbole* is literally in general terms excess.

In rhetoric it is an exaggeration, something which speaks of something in excessive terms.

In geometry it is another conic section formed by the intersection of a plane with both branches of a cone, in which the inclination of the cutting plane to the axis ***exceeds*** that of the cone's side. (*as seen on the next page*)

An '*ellipsis*' is literally a falling short, a deficiency.

In rhetoric, it denotes the omission from a clause of one or more words needed to complete the sense – the utterance thus falls short of completion.

In geometry it is a conic section in which the cutting plane's inclination *is less* than – falls short of – the inclination of the cone's side".[10] (*as seen below*)

That is the most powerful proof, in my opinion, that mathematics and literature are rooted in the human soil and are for good and for bad eternally inter-connected

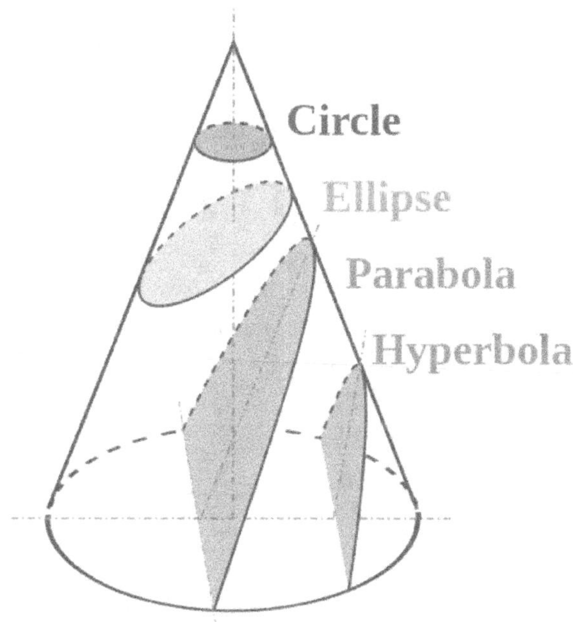

---

[10] Carey, B. (2014). *How We Learn. The Surprising Truth about When, Where, and Why It Happens,* pp. 36. Random House LLC. Halinen, I. (2015). "General Aspects of Basic Education Curriculum Reform 2016 Finland." Retrieved on July 12, 2015.

1.3 Bibliotherapy

As a part of expressive therapy, bibliotherapy is based on the premise of the healing, consoling power of a book. The basis of bibliotherapy is rooted in the psychology of reading and the "book / reader" interaction. In bibliotherapy, the value of literature depends strictly on its capacity to encourage a therapeutic response from the participants. The individual's feeling-response is more important than an intellectual grasp of the work's meaning. In a way it is a form of self-administered treatment in which structured materials provide a means to alleviate distress. The concept of the treatment is based on the human inclination to identify themselves with others through their expressions in literature and art. For instance, a grieving child who reads, or is read a story about another child who has lost a parent may feel less alone in the world.

The Online Dictionary for Library and Information Science (2011) defines bibliotherapy as:

"The use of books selected on the basis of content in a planned reading program designed to facilitate the recovery of patients suffering from mental illness or emotional disturbance.

Ideally, the process occurs in three phases:

a. Personal identification of the reader with a particular character in the recommended work resulting in
b. Psychological catharsis, when the reader shares many of the same thoughts and feelings of the characters in the literary work
c. Rational insight concerning the relevance of the solution suggested in the text to the reader's own experience"[11].

---

[11] Lehr, Fran. (1981). Bibliotherapy. *Journal of Reading*, 25.

And there is a lot of bibliotherapy going on these days, as it was through the history.

The results are well documented and the growing anxiety of the modern civilization makes bibliotherapy a more and more attractive option if not a compulsive action for all of us, not only for those that have a medical condition.

Hence bibliotherapy in a larger, lighter sense is a therapy for each of us, as we all have some sort of angst of a kind. It seems that the desire to read is inoculated in our DNA – although some of us might not have felt that desire yet – a desire to read and imagine what we read, to travel in time and space, dive, immerse in other realities, fictional worlds of adventures and loyalty…and guess what? With books there is no "forced sociability" … As one famous bibliotherapist said, if we pass the evening with those friends – books that is – it's because we really want to. When we leave them, we do so with regret and, when we have left them, there are none of those thoughts that spoil friendship: 'What did they think of us?' – 'Did we make a mistake and say something tactless?' – 'Did they like us?' – nor is there the anxiety of being forgotten because of displacement by someone else. And that does not say – by all means – that we become less sociable.

"A book in need is a friend indeed". The healing effect of the books has been by now superfluously documented from both a medical and philosophical perspective.

But it seems that there is no explanation as to why actually that is, why that healing effect is triggered or shaped.

And here is what I think.

Since almost two hundred years, literature, music, cinematography preached and conveyed us we have to live and love the most we can, as at the end of the day, nothing else will count apart from this intensity of life we lived. There seem to be only one principle for the modern life in that the Self is directing for itself: everything that shall happen should happen with glowing heart, with intensity. Surely moral values (dignity, loyalty, respect, don't cheat, don't steal…) will always prevail, based on which the actions and the whole existence of a human being can be seen as good or bad. Yet, this morality is slowly replaced by an inner intense ethic, which infiltrates in people's hearts and affects their thinking about the value of one's life.

And maybe we can talk even about an "aristocratic" ethic (in the sense that the true aristocrats are not noble by the name they have attached, but by their behavior) in our democratic societies in that we do not judge any longer over the content of a behavior, we should rather judge the excellence of the manifestation of that behavior and value its intensity.

Now, reading is exactly that, it is generating that intensity in ourselves in the best way possible, and gives us this feeling of pulsing life. If it is an historic novel, a love story, a hate story, a magic reality South American narrative, a poem about destiny and unfulfilled love, or a machiavellic parable, if hero or villain, if it is about the solitude of prime numbers or the discovery of time – it does not matter … the cause of the excitement, is surely important, but the actual intensity of our feeling is what counts at most, what really matters.

"What remains invariable may be possibly true, but it is not alive. What is simple, safe, static and remains unchanged is surely satisfying parts of our mind – but these are the amorphous parts –, yet it is degrading in ourselves the awareness of Life, the Intensity of Life"[12].

---

[12] Tristan Garcia. *The intensive Life.*

Existential intensity, that is what we are all longing for …

So, go and grab a book and read, try some mathematics or play piano, live, feel the intensity of Life and get healed of your boredom, laziness, angst and mistrust!!!

What is the problem?

Well, we seem to know the problem…in theory.

We know about not eating too much, about being kind, about getting to bed early, about focusing on our opportunities before it is too late, about the importance, excitement and the pulsing intensity of our feelings generated by reading a book. And yet in practice, our wise ideas have a notoriously weak ability to motivate our actual behavior. Our knowledge is both embedded within us and yet is ineffective for us.

The Ancient Greeks were unusually alert to this phenomenon and gave it a helpfully resonant name: akrasia, commonly translated as 'weakness of will'. It was, they proposed, because of akrasia that we have such a tragic inclination for knowing what to do but not acting upon our own best principles.

But more about that, if you are interested, is in the attached paper or you may find out in my next lecture.

1.4 Conclusions – things to take away

1. Matter and energy are intrinsically linked to each other, so science and humanities, so mathematics and literature and music… Through the humanities we reflect on the fundamental question: What does it mean to be human? And yes, humanities offer clues but never

a complete answer. They reveal how people have tried to make moral, spiritual, and intellectual sense of a world where irrationality, despair, loneliness, and death are as conspicuous as birth, friendship, hope, and reason. But as we know, the modern mantra is that everything is related to everything and anything can change everything, therefore the desire to link humanities with science is more a duty than a necessity.

2. Human brain does not think in disciplines, it was trained to do so in the last few centuries; we understand processes and phenomena and the ways our body, brain and soul works is by its nature holistic. That is why, maybe, the modern school teaching nowadays is not based on disciplines any longer, it is rather phenomenon based learning (PBL)[9] and shows us the path to the future of our evolution.

3. In contemporary culture, many people value things, including scientific knowledge, according to how practical they are. What we don't always realize is that while we are wishing for a scientific notion to be useful in a tangible way, what we really want is for it to be relevant to our lives in a way that may contribute to giving a sense and fulfilling our existence. The most important thing about the Theory of General Relativity is not that it enables us to use GPS systems (which are pretty useful nonetheless, one would consider); rather, it is important because it is fascinating to grasp it. To transform our minds to understand that, as far as we know, space can be curved and the flow of time can be altered by the effect of mass – it is a challenge beyond our rationale power, which we should embrace. In this sense, math and literature can be measured with the same "subjective" ruler – intensity or the level of fascination of that intensity – although, weirdly enough, the intensity of its relevance to our lives, or the intensity and fascination of enriching our lives will always remain a personal experience, immeasurable and hence sublime and divine.

You should actually draw your own conclusions and even if it were only thoughtfulness and contemplation that my words generated – I would consider my job done.

Thank you for your patience and attention.

1.5 References

1. Rick Szostak – Defining interdisciplinarity
   https://sites.google.com/a/ualberta.ca/rick-szostak/research/about-interdisciplinarity/definitions/defining-instrumental-interdisciplinarity
2. *Matthew Wickman – Literature after Euclid, Haney foundation*
3. *Lehr, Fran. (1981). Bibliotherapy. Journal of Reading, 25*
4. *Tristan Garcia – The intensive Life*
5. *Jorge Alejandro Laris Pardo – „Infinities in literature and mathematics"*
6. *Emmer M, Quarteroni Mathknow, Vol 3 – Springer Verlag Italia 2009*
7. *https://www.bu.edu/wcp/Papers/Aest/AestGilm.htm*
8. *https://english.stackexchange.com*
9. *Carey, B. (2014). How We Learn: The Surprising Truth about When, Where, and Why It Happens, pp. 36. Random House LLC. Hallnen, I. (2015). "General Aspects of Basic Education Curriculum Reform 2016 Finland." Retrieved on July 12, 2015*

Bettering Humanity through Biology

Manuel Galvão de Melo e Mota

Biology is arguably referred to as the "science of the XXIth century". This prestigious title intrinsically contains a huge responsibility. For many centuries, Biology has contributed directly or indirectly to bettering humankind, although its obvious and objective effects have only been made evident since the XIXth century. There are three main domains to which Biology has made significant contributions: Agriculture, Environment and Medicine. Several scientific disciplines connected to Biology have been involved such as Genetics (mendelian and molecular), Cell Biology, Ecology, Microbiology, and what was known for a long time as "Natural History" (today we would include these roughly within Botany and Zoology). Agronomy, a relatively recent science, has made a tremendous impact by providing knowledge on growing plants and animals, and developing new and better crops. One specific moment in time, following WW II, known as the "Green Revolution" benefitted humanity immensely, by combating hunger in countries such as India and Mexico. The "father" of the Green Revolution, Norman Borlaug, was awarded the 1970 Peace Nobel Prize for such achievements. In the XXIth century, biologists and agronomists are working hard to develop new and better crops to feed almost 8 billion people. In the medical field, the contributions are inumerable, from the discovery and development of vaccines (Jenner and Pasteur), to antibiotics (Fleming) and combatting diseases. This has increased the average life expectancy of humans from around 30-40 in the beginning of the XXth century, to a present value of around 75 (depending on the country). These achievements have been recognized by society, through dozens of Nobel Prizes in Medicine. All these successes have been made possible through Biology. In the past 30-40 years, numerous voices have been raised alerting for the environmental degradation of our planet, its land and oceans, its biomes and ecosystems. We have been depleting our planet at an incredible rate. But today, biologists and environmental scientists have the knowledge and tools to better the planet. We know how the ecosystems function and what causes harm them. There is still time, together with a strong public opinion, to halt the damage. Once again, Biology is a principal actor.

1. Introduction

Throughout the ages, biological science has made tremendous contributions to bettering Humanity. In the IVth century BC, Aristotle was aware of the advantages and contributions that the natural sciences provided, from the purely scientific point of view to the empowerment of politicians (he was firstly advisor do king Philip II of Macedonia, and later teacher and mentor of Alexander the Great).

Naturalists and medical doctors (although at the time it would be hard to distinguish between both) were frequently requested and hired by kings and other rulers, throughout the world, be it Rome or China. Perhaps one of the famous cases would be the Greek-born Galen, who functioned as the imperial doctor of several Roman emperors.

All through Humanity's History, it is clear that rulers at large, and even most countries' populations, were aware of the fantastic contributions that knowledge and practices with a biological background make to better peoples' lives. These can be broadly characterized under Agriculture, Environment and Medicine. It is also interesting to observe the close relationship that these developments and this progress were closely associated with technical improvements, physical or chemical, for example the development of the microscope, or the identification and development of pharmaceutical compounds.

2. Agriculture

Very early on, let's say several thousands of years BC, when human being changed from a hunter-gatherer mode of life to a more sedentary agricultural entity, it became clear that he was able to domesticate plants and animals and provide a more varied diet to feed his family and tribe, as well as to breed animals for all sorts of activities; all this was very empirical, of course, but it was a beginning. Even around 4000 BC, one is stunned by the magnificent engraving found in present-day Iraq, displaying a pedigree showing the transmission of characteristics through five generations of horses (Fig. 1).

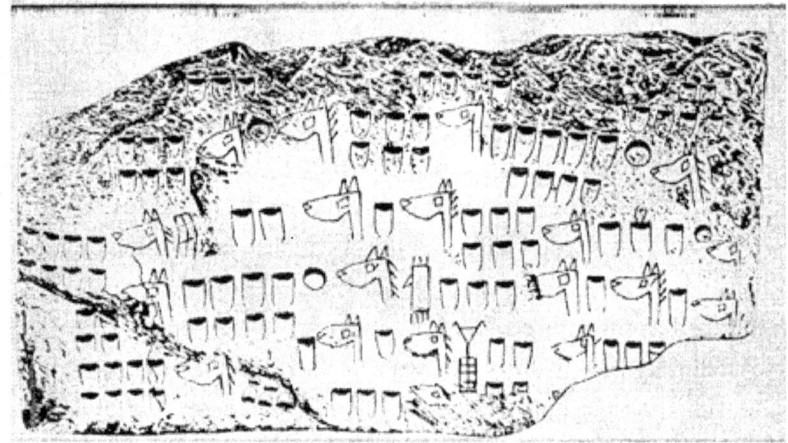

Fig. 1 – W. Amschler – 1935

The domestication of numerous crops took place throughout the Neolithic period, all through ancient Egypt, Greece and Rome. The early civilizations were in fact located in an area known as the "fertile crescent", which we know today is the center of origin of a large number of crop species, namely cereals.

Knowledge of crop as well as medicinal and aromatic plants was greatly expanded in the XVIth century, with the first globalization power, Portugal, who brought back to Europe thousands of plants and animals unknown (at the time). Garcia de Orta, who spent most of his time in Goa (India), stands out as the pioneer and most important botanist of the time. This wealth of knowledge, continued by many other explorers and naturalists, from Spain, France, England, The Netherlands and others would be paramount for the foundations of modern plant classification (Linaeus, XVIIIth century), plant domestication, and agriculture.

The biological foundations of plant breeding (until then a more or less empirical activity) were laid down by an Augustinian monk living in the city of Brno, now Czech Republic (at the time, around 1850, it was the Moravian region of the Austro-Hungarian Empire). His name: Gregor Mendel (Fig. 2):

Fig. 2 – Gregor Mendel

The famous pea experiments resulted in an understanding of the basic, simple principles of hereditary transmission, which later became known as the science of Genetics.

The early XXth century, besides the "re-discovery" of Mendel's laws of inheritance, saw an extraordinary expansion of the biological knowledge which provided basis for a betterment of new crops and animals. The exact location of genes, responsible for providing the characteristics of all plants and animals (as well as of microbes), culminating in the discovery of the physical structure of the DNA molecule (Watson & Crick, 1953) (Fig. 3), made it possible to cross-breed and develop better and more productive plants and animals. This became evident following World War II, when Humanity drastically needed to feed a desperate population of survivors, as well as of millions of destitute people around the world.

Fig. 3 – DNA Model by Watson & Crick

A central figure here is Norman Borlaug (Fig. 4), who made extraordinary experiments in plant breeding, with cereals (mainly wheat), creating new and much more productive varieties, saving the lives of millions, especially in Mexico, India and the far East. This was known as the "Green Revolution". For his vast achievements, he received the 1970 Nobel Peace Prize.

Fig. 4 – Norman Borlaug

Borlaug's work has been steadily continued throughout the XXth century, and now in the XXIth century, with modern plant biotechnology, establishing new varieties of plants, more productive and protected against pests and pathogens. Today, nearly 2 billion ha of biotech crops (as they became known), such as soybean, maize, cotton, rice (the famous "golden rice"), tomato and so on, have been planted throughout the world (Fig. 5). This new "green revolution" has brought with it concerns in terms of food safety and security, but humans have been capable of evaluating the risks of these GM.

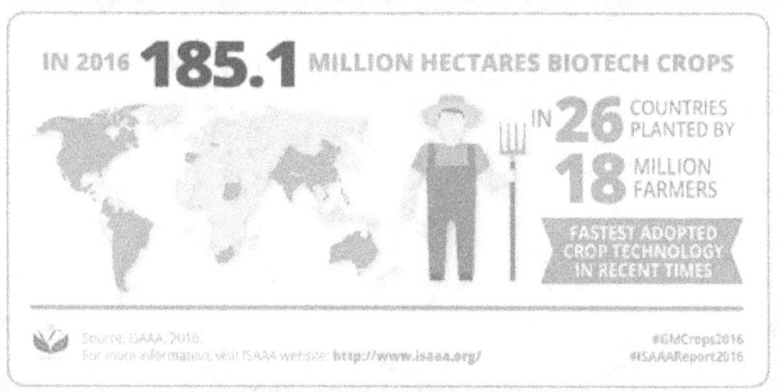

Fig. 5 – GM Crops

In summary, Biology has been central to the main discoveries related to the agricultural sciences (plant crops and domestic animals), and has contributed to the bettering of humanity, feeding it at a steady rate, with better, more productive and healthier products, such as cereals, milk and meat, to mention just a few examples.

3. *Environment*

Perhaps the most recent scientific branch, or application related to Biology is Environmental Science, or Ecology. The prefix "eco" derives from the Greek "oikos", which means "home", and in fact our planet, and more specifically the Biosphere, is our home.

For centuries, perhaps without realizing it, humanity adapted to its "home", but without understanding the need to keep it in good shape. In pristine days, most of the planet was unexplored, virgin in many ways, with forestas, mountains, etc… still kept in balance with the animal populations including the human species.

It is estimated that only around 200 million people lived around the year 1 AD. The first billion (thousand of million) people was reached only in 1800, and only nearly 200 years later we are now almost 8 billion people.

When the Portuguese arrived in Brasil in 1500, the coastal area was furrowed in a lush mantle of forests known as the "Mata Atlântica" (Atlantic Forest). Today, it is residual (Fig. 6).

Fig. 6 – Atlantic Forest

The geometrical population growth since 1800, coupled with devastating wars, in Europe but elsewhere, have brought increasing pressure to the environment and to the numerous terrestrial and aquatic ecosystems. But for a long time this went basically unnoticed. Practically no one, not even the brightest scientists of the XIXth century, even those close to the "Romantic" movement, raised any concern or alerts regarding the environment.

In the mid- and late XIX century, the Industrial Revolution put extraordinary pressure on the major European cities. Rural populations flocked to the industrial centers where jobs and money was available. Slowly, people started realizing the issues related to this sudden social change. Early pioneers in the conservationist movement included the famous American naturalist and philosopher Henry David Thoreau (1817-1862), but the first great contribution to the environment and concern for humans, came with John Muir (1838-1914) (Fig. 7) who in 1892 founded the Sierra Club, still active today.

Fig. 7 – John and Teddy

One of his famous statements was: *"Keep close to nature's heart, and break clear away, once in a while, and climb a mountain or spend a week in the woods. Wash your spirit clean"*. How modern and ahead of his time! Muir had a powerful ally in this quest, President Theodore Roosevelt; it was early in his presidency (1901) that Roosevelt created the United States Forest Service, and the Natural Parks (150 national forests) and 5 Great National Parks. The pioneer US system constituted a model for all major natural parks around the world. He stated then: *"We have fallen heirs to the most glorious heritage a people ever received, and each one must do his part if we wish to show that the nation is worthy of its good fortune"*.

Despite the rapid and powerful developments of the Western world's XXth century, Muir's message was not forgotten. Aldo Leopold (1887-1948) became a new pioneer for the last century, by writing abundantly about Nature and Man, and establishing the contrasting views "Eco-Ego". But world had undergone two major conflicts, in 1914-1918 and 1939-1945, so concerns with the environment took a back seat in the priorities of countries and rulers who needed to solve hunger problems; a time when huge amounts of pesticides and other agro-chemicals were used. The alarm sounded in 1962 with the famous Rachel Carson book "Silent Spring".

In the 1970s, and having the US as a pioneer country, a series of legislative initiatives such as , e.g., the "Clean Air Act", "Earth Day", etc... followed by a series of important international conferences (Stockholm, 1972; Montreal, 1987; Rio, 1992; Kyoto, 1997; and more recently Copenhagen, 2009) consolidated a strong environmental and conservationist movement which lasts until today.

Biologists and ecologists have been playing a pivotal role in providing the know-how and research which is paramount for decision makers. Zoologist Edward Wilson (Fig. 8), from Harvard University, has contributed immensely to our knowledge on Biodiversity, and the need to conserve it. Scientists working on sensitive and iconic ecosystems such as the Amazon rainforest or the Galapagos Islands have provided help in making the planet a better place to live.

Fig. 8 – Edward Wilson

4. Medicine

Since the early ages of the human species, its health has been a central concern; firstly to protect the family and the tribe, in a very empirical and primitive form, and later on in a more organized fashion, with the emergence of specialists in different areas of the medical science.

From mysticism to the scientific revolution of the XVIIth century, all kinds of "witch doctors", surgeons, dentists, etc... did their best to heal wounds and suffering. But the lack of proper instruments and above all a mental and scientific framework in all societies, hindered progress. The microscope (van Leuwenhoek and Hooke, ca.1665) made a decisive contribution, namely in bettering our knowledge of human anatomy, still stuck in the old anatomies of Galen and Vesalius. An understanding of the human blood circulation, e.g., by Harvey in England (1628, *"De motus cordi"*) and a demonstration made to King Charles I, very impressive events at the time. New surgical methods could now be implemented, bettering operations and the chance of survival.

Another good example of a major contribution is vaccination. A simple country doctor, Edward Jenner (1749-1823), observed that the ladies who were milking cows, which suffered from what was then known as "cow pox" were apparently free from developing the disease, and developed in their arms smaller pustules, which he named "small pox" (until today, as referred as "variola"). By applying a diluted shot of these pustules to a young suffering boy, he became cured very quickly.

It took more than 50 years for this technique (thought at the time by the general public as crazy) to become scientifically established, by the man who founded modern Microbiology, Louis Pasteur (1822-1895) (Fig. 9).

Fig. 9 – Louis Pasteur 1885

The contributions of this biologist to the bettering of humanity are infinite, from the study of crystals (enantiomers) (1847), understanding the chemical basis of fermentation (1857), definitely refuting the "spontaneous generation" theory (1860), saving France's silk industry from disease and destruction (1865-1870), it's cattle industry from anthrax (1877-1881) and the establishment of the rabies vaccine. His legacy has been kept until today, with the establishment of the Pasteur Institute, a major research institute which today provides all kinds of vaccines, such as e.g. against the various flu epidemics.

Microbiology indeed has been a major area in Biology, as well as medical science, where more contributions have been made to provide humans with a longer and better life. Such is the case of penicillin and all the later antibiotics, initiated in 1928 by Alexander Fleming (1881-1955). Or, more recently, the discovery of the polio vaccine by Jonas Salk (1914-1995) (Fig. 10), who saved the lives of millions of children.

Fig. 10 – Jonas Salk

Present day scientific domains within Biology, such as immunology to understand and treat diseases such as lupus and other auto-immune diseases, or the use of stem cells, to treat Alzheimer's disease or stroke, or the area of reproductive biology, where new discoveries and techniques of embryonic development, have been able to provide infertile parents with children, have made tremendous contributions to bettering humanity. There is no question about this.

The Eye in Ideas: Culture, Curiosity and Communication in Scientific Discovery

Nigel Sanitt

How is meaning created in science and what part do questions play in scientific theories? Many aspects of research activity in science are opaque to outsiders and this opacity infects how connections are made between science and other disciplines. We have this tremendous feeling that science has progressed, which has resulted in technological advancement beyond anything we have seen before. The only blemish on this scenario is that the foundations of science seem to be built on sand. Theories come and go and truth is elusive to understanding, even a hindrance. Knowledge acquisition appears to be an end in itself, as though knowledge is some sort of commodity or object that can be traded. We have created a mythical objective world, where we pretend that opinions and values are generated by data alone and not by people, or worse scientists. Scientists bask in the new technological Atlantis, oblivious to the mismatch between quantum mechanics and general relativity – our two most important physical theories, and revelling in the fact that the nature of most of the matter in the universe is anybody's guess. Science is part of our culture and part of the understanding of science now, and in the past, is bound up with recognising the social, economic and political ramifications as they apply to science. In this article I put forward a radical interpretation of how science works to address these questions and try to put science in its rightful context of a means of helping us to engage with our world.

1.1 Introduction

Most people are not artists or musicians but that does not mean that they cannot look at an oil painting or hear a piece of music and appreciate the beauty. Science is a little different. Most people have not studied medicine or astrophysics, but that does not mean that they don't appreciate it when a physician cures them of acne or they enjoy watching a film of a simulation of two black holes colliding.

We have this tremendous feeling that science has progressed, which has resulted in technological advancement beyond anything we have seen before. Even distinguishing technological progress from pure scientific progress, we have more theories and better theories. The only blemish on this scenario is that the foundations of science seem to be uncertain. Theories come and go and truth is elusive to understanding, even a hindrance. Knowledge acquisition appears to be an end in itself, as though knowledge is some sort of commodity or object that can be traded. We have created an objective world, where we pretend that opinion and values are generated by data alone and not by people, or worse scientists. Scientists bask in the new technological Atlantis, oblivious to the mismatch between quantum mechanics and general relativity – our two most prominent physical theories, and reveling in the fact that the nature of most of the matter in the universe is anybody's guess.

Are scientists up in arms about these problems? Are they coming together across all disciplines to remedy the situation? The answers to both of these questions are yes and no. There is a fair amount of hand wringing and shrugging of shoulders – yes, it is quite difficult to do both of these actions at the same time! Much lip service is paid to cross disciplinary studies, but most scientists plough their own furrow; granted, usually within a larger group of co-workers. In many cases interdisciplinarity has given way to compartmentalization and genuine communication is missing from the process of science. Even large groups that collectively engage in outreach, comprise one or two scientists. Although some involve specialist communicators who are brought in to out-source these functions, which the grant-awarding organizations have required.

There are a huge number of players and organizations involved in the scientific process. Not all of these individuals and groups are scientists, or even know much about science. This is not to denigrate hard-working, behind the scenes administrators, civil servants and other specialists. Science is a collective enterprise and scientists, though central, are only one cog in the whole machine. So, what is the use of this endeavour we call science? Where does it lead? What is the outcome? I remember once being in a seminar given by a well-known scientist, who was explaining at length complex calculations on galactic dynamics and early star formation.[1] At the end of the lecture someone from the audience asked the question: What is the result of your calculation? The lecturer thought for a few seconds and then replied: Stars!

Science predicts. At the end of the day when we switch on some new electrical gadget we want to know that it will work and that it will do "what it says on the tin". In a more general sense, science enables us to calculate consequences. In this respect science is no more nor less than an extension of our innate human ability to cope with and engage the physical world around us – a world that also includes ourselves. So how do we make sense of the world? Wisdom, knowledge and language imply that we have some sort of idea of the meaning of meaning. We cannot put ourselves outside language and ask what we mean when we say something; by language I not only refer to the spoken or written word, but also non-verbal language and language cues. Science, in common with other disciplines is not just about what is written in books, articles and papers. Those published words are a distillation of only a fraction of work that scientists perform, which is deemed publishable. That is why it is vital for researchers to communicate with each other, attend seminars and conferences and

---

[1] Donald Lynden-Bell.

become "linked in" with those working in their subject. Acquisition of such hidden knowledge, opinions, ideas and prejudices is part of the whole process of science.

1.2 Meaning and question networks

Meaning itself is hardly ever discussed by scientists. Scientists are concerned with explanation and understanding, rather than meaning. Scientists can sometimes have a somewhat Humpty Dumpty[2] attitude:

*"When I use a word, ... it means just what I choose it to mean –
neither more nor less."*

Meaning changes with time and is socially and culturally affected. Many scientific theories employ quantities which have no relationship with everyday objects. This is part of the power of science that unfamiliar concepts can be incorporated into our view of the world. It is also part of the problem that metaphorical language can be pushed to the point of hindering understanding. Hindrances are myths which we create such as: words correspond to objects in the world, or we can communicate mental states directly to each other. I promote the theory that meaning is integrational, that we acquire meaning by integrating our actions communally with others. Language, ideas, memories, and prejudices all combine to create meaning. We are all embedded in this network of meaning, which itself, changes and evolves over time.

Curiosity is a significant characteristic of our species. In fact, many species exhibit curiosity, even though we are the only one that

---

[2] Fictional character from *Through the Looking-Glass* (1872) by Lewis Carroll (1832-1898)

uses language – we ask questions. Question-asking is essential to us in everyday life, but as far as science is concerned asking questions, particularly open-ended questions, is a signal feature of the scientific process. I go one step further: questions are fundamental to scientific theorising and the problematological network is what defines theories in science. As far as curiosity is concerned, it is a drive which defines what it is to be a living entity. Clearly, single-celled organisms do not ask questions, but if one thinks of curiosity as part of a spectrum, with basic exploratory behaviour at one end and scientific or intellectual curiosity at the other, then one can draw together all these strands of behaviour under one explanation. All life has to engage with its environment and without the curiosity spectrum, time and the second law of thermodynamics; it would render the whole enterprise of life otiose.

As far as open-ended scientific questions are concerned, there are two kinds: empirical and theoretical. Empirical questions rest on a nexus of presuppositions and other questions and answers, which form a closed system for the researcher. I refer to this as black-boxing. Theoretical questions are generated by empirical questions and answers, which lead to a problematological network. The distinction between empirical and theoretical questions is one of choice, with strings, for the questioner.

Black boxes can be opened up at any time and a flood of questions released. This happens because scientists generally work within a consensus and presuppositions, assumptions and vales are held communally. Scientists who try to open a black box have to have a good reason and the threshold for success is usually extremely high. There is no *truth* in science and one of the paramount features of questions is that a question cannot be true or false. It is this characteristic that makes questions ideal candidates to be the invariants in scientific theories.

There is more to science than just theories. All scientists work at trying to experiment, observe, question and think about how to probe nature's secrets. The theoretical framework is desirable but sometimes it is just not there. In those situations, researchers fall back on partial theories, half-baked ideas and sometimes sheer grit and determination. The interesting point is what divides scientific theories from partial theories and half-baked ideas? This is referred to as the demarcation problem.

In the scheme I present, theories are built up as networks of questions and answers. Empirical and theoretical questions are represented by logical links which form a problematological network. It is, however, not enough to say that a theory is a network. If that were it, then I would be guilty of overusing a metaphor, a sin which I have previously identified. To put meat on the bone, there has to be more than just the analogy: "theories are networks". The networks I refer to have rules. There are two main restrictions. First, tautological or mathematical elements of theories are not part of the question and answer matrix and are excluded. Second, theories and the networks representing them have to exhibit progress: they have to create some gain in the knowledge we have of the world. The way this is incorporated into the system is to say that empirical questions must outweigh in number theoretical questions, which have been created. The result is a matrix of understanding driven by experimentation, observation and cogitation. A crucial consequence of these rules is in the definition of progress, which impacts on the demarcation problem. What happens when a question and answer network covers insufficient empirical questions to count as a theory? – there are too many theoretical questions. The answer is that what is created is a partial theory or a half-baked idea. The world of science is full of these, some may grow into proper theories, most will end up in the dustbin of science.

Theories are thus our created response to the world; they are not objects which are "out there" in some Platonic sense, but frameworks we use to model nature. The network model has a ready-made mathematical expression in *graph theory*.[3] This is a branch of mathematics where relationships between abstract entities are represented by links and nodes, which are referred to as edges and vertices. This is a common example where mathematical formalism fits neatly into applications in nature.

We can list all the network rules and characteristics together with the corresponding graph theory analogues as in Table 1.

TABLE 1

Comparison between scientific theory rules and graph theory analogues

Scientific Theories	Graph Theory
Specific Theory	Connected graph of vertices and directed edges
Questions	Vertices
Relations between questions	Directed edges
Exclude Truth	Acyclic[4] digraph
Empirical questions outnumber theoretical questions	Width[5] greater than half the number of vertices

It never ceases to amaze me when advanced mathematical structures find applications in unexpected and diverse areas. This is relevant to the idea of beauty in science and mathematics. Graph theory is the

---

[3] Not to be confused with x-y Cartesian graphs, where two variables are plotted against each other.

[4] If you follow nodes and directed vertices around a graph and come back to your starting point then that corresponds to a cycle. Directed graphs without a cycle are acyclic.

[5] The width is the number of source vertices representing empirical questions.

mathematical model for representing relationships between abstract quantities. One of the possible theories behind the quest for a new theory of quantum gravity is loop quantum gravity. In this theory time and space are secondary to abstract combinatorial structures described by graphs. At the present time no one knows what kind of theory of quantum gravity lies on the horizon, but whatever form it takes, I would be surprised if graph theory did not play some part – in physics, beauty is much more than skin deep.

1.3 Communication

There are a number of aspects of science which come under the general heading of communication. At a straightforward level, there is communication between scientists and the public, covered by terms such as outreach, public understanding of science and science communication. Beyond this narrow version of communication, there is encroachment into the political and economic arenas with public relations and work done by press officers, policy advisers and lobbyists. Large scientific international experimental projects have also spurred the need for specialists liaising with grant-awarding bodies. Universities' alumni organisations are a conduit, not only for large sums donated for research and expansion, but also for universities keeping in close contact with their former students. Scientist on scientist communication is also vital. Certainly, in a wider multidisciplinary world, scientists need to know what is happening outside of their own subject area, but also within a particular discipline, intercommunication is crucial and impacts directly on the research process. In the political sphere there is usually a mismatch between timescales, with scientists planning projects over decades and politicians only concerned with the period to the next election. To be fair, this problem is appreciated by most politicians but with wider economic exigencies to contend with politicians and civil servants only pay lip service to the dictum that science cannot be turned on and off as a tap.

I consider three examples where evolving communication patterns give rise to both positive and negative outcomes: Medicine, Climate change and Africa. Communication in medicine has always had particular problems because there are two kinds of languages involved. Physicians have to communicate with their patients as well as each other, and they cannot use a common idiom with both groups. This problem has become exacerbated in two ways in recent years. First, the great strides in medical imaging techniques has resulted in the unintended consequence of too many irregularities turning up in medical scans, which are ultimately non-threatening, but which cause great anxiety to patients. Second, the advent of the internet has made medical information so readily available that it has created the phenomenon of Dr Google, where patients inform their physicians of what they have found on the web about their medical condition.

Communication with governments and the public on climate change has changed since the problem was first mooted. At the beginning, the uneven costs for countries in tackling the problem, resulted in no overall consensus with a division of countries into a north south split. As an international consensus started to emerge, with the aim of confronting the problem in a sustainable and fairer way, the debate has shifted from win loss to win win.

The problems in Africa are still work in progress. A bright spot is the positive effects of the internet and mobile communications. As these become generally more available, and given Africa's demography of increasing urbanisation and young population, the outlook for the continent is promising.

1.4 Culture

Science is part of our culture and one area where there is a healthy interchange of ideas is literature. I use the term loosely to include the arts: fiction writing, poetry, theatre, film, TV, music and video games. Literature and science contribute to each other: both ask questions. Fiction creates possible futures and many works of fiction have scientific themes. These range from direct applications of a future science as in the science fiction genre, to a subtler scientific background. Poetry and song lyrics may sometimes use metaphorical language to represent science. The interface between science and literature covers two agendas. First, there may be a direct scientific motif; a fictional world which confronts an audience with possible scenarios, based on science present and potential. The other possibility is that science may be represented in a purely metaphorical way where language is used in a way that links an audience with scientific subject matter on a different level. This is particularly, though not exclusively, a characteristic of poetry writing, either within a poem or a song lyric.

There are some branches of physics, especially quantum theory, where poetic language can resonate in a meaningful way and encourage understanding to a degree that narrative prose doesn't quite reach. A small but significant number of scientists also write novels and poetry. Many of them are inspired by their scientific work.

Religion and science have been intertwined for centuries in a cultural, social and political mêlée that has not always been uneventful or beneficial. The simple attitude, shared by many scientists, is that fact and faith do not mix; therefore, religion has nothing to do with science. Add to that the claim that religion is about truth, and in science truth is excluded, then that supports the attitude. On the other hand, both science and religion are more complex, they are not just about truth and faith versus facts. There are three particular areas where science benefits from a strong interaction with religious ideas. First, religion generates ideas. The question asked by Thales two thousand six hundred years ago of what one entity is the world made of and notions of unity, right up to the present-day preoccupation with a theory of everything, are all testament to the fruitfulness of religious ideas – science owes religion this debt. Second, the philosophical, psychological and AI debate on the existence of free will is informed by religious arguments. Third, if religion is about anything, it is about how people, including scientists, ought to behave. Moral ideas, including how science should be conducted, are informed by religious and ethical norms. These may certainly be couched in the form of secular practices, but it cannot be avoided that historically, religious ideas are the precursors of ethical behaviour.

According to the old adage, a picture is worth a thousand words. This is particularly the case in science. Whether it is a photograph, a drawing, an oil painting or a sculpture, images are central to science. There is a two-way street involved with visual art; enhancing scientific understanding and science experimentation providing the means of artistic expression. Behind both tracks is notion of beauty, which is just as much a core feature in science as in art. This is a throwback to Plato, in that some art claims to depict an ideal, a Platonic form. This aspect of art is at the present time more common to scientists than artists, who have moved on from art as static depiction (mimesis), with art, instead of just picturing the world, represents objects, ideas and processes in time and space. The situation is changing and in science museums and scientists' engagement with the public, the art of the visual is seen more and more as a means of communicating science. By moving away from art as mimesis, science displays can utilise visual media as a means of explaining and publicising science in novel ways.

The arts and sciences are complex systems. Complex systems have a number of features, including extreme sensitivity to initial conditions: small perturbations are amplified by feedback, and have a huge range of possible outcomes which are, in practice, impossible to predict. Such chaotic behaviour describes life, including human beings. Humans, in common with all life, have to engage with the world and cope with everyday problems. How we think and make decisions is something which has been honed over countless generations. It is sometimes, quite literally, a matter of life and death to rapidly make the right decision.

1.5 Thinking

One theory, which reflects this decision process, describes a series or spectrum of information available for us to make decisions. The simple end of this sequence corresponds to the gist or basic summary of a problem situation. The other end of the spectrum follows increasing detail, leading to an advanced verbatim account of what is being faced. How we react and solve any problem is a question of how far up this spectrum we want to go, given the limited time available we might have. Most decisions utilise the gist of a problem, and in the case of the public's reaction to climate change problems for example, we can see this effect in that beyond a certain point, more data does not affect the public's viewpoint, as much as a change in the way the subject is reported by journalists.

One description of our thinking process is as an emergent property of our brains. A property of complex systems is the notion of emergence. This is when there is a hierarchy of levels, which produce patterns and order at the highest level. Another theory, and the one I promote here, is that thinking is an active voluntary process, most of which we learn to do. Consciousness arises out of the level of perception we attend to. Similar to the spectrum of detail we focus on when we have to make decisions, so consciousness comes into play when we move into a middle zone of brain and body engagement with our environment. Consciousness thus trumps everything else in how we decide to act. The brain, body and environment can't be split up. In trying to mimic the mind in AI research, the problem is how to decide when to stop thinking; in other words, at what point on the spectrum do you sit?

The *golden rule* dominates ethical and moral behaviour: *"do unto others as you would have them do unto you."* But in a complex world with science impacting more and more our daily lives, ethical and moral considerations on the part of scientists is of major importance. Beyond Mertonian principles of equality, fairness in publication, objectivity and scepticism, scientists have to be vigilant against falsehood and the perversion of the scientific process. When there are large sums of research money and high reputation involved, the heady mix is a temptation to the weak and incompetent to engage in misconduct. The first Mertonian principle is equality. Unfortunately, especially in the physical sciences, the proportion of female students is small. Granted, the situation has improved over recent decades, but there is still a long way to go.

For a minority of scientists, philosophy and science are separated by a chasm. With many scientists having to become involved in many multidisciplinary projects and the encroachment of science into other disciplines, such an attitude is indefensible. A lack of critical thinking skills leads to intellectual impoverishment and in the end – poor science. There are many universities that include philosophy courses in their undergraduate science curriculum – this is to be encouraged.

I have culled ideas, explanations and theories from a wide range of disciplines as they apply to scientific theories and practices. I want to bring all the threads together in a unified way. Not all the threads are as different from each other as they first appear, but refer to similar situations seen from alternative viewpoints. I am reminded of the story of the blind men and the elephant. Each one feels one part, such as the leg or the trunk and then describes the object. All the descriptions disagree with each other. Life is the process of our engagement with the world, a part of which is what we refer to as science. We do science all the time and in many different guises, but certain advanced aspects have become formalised into what we call the physical sciences. But the cultural, social and political characteristics are still present, though secluded.

A Truly Knowledgeable Person must first be an Attentive Questioner

João Miguel Pais & Maria Burguete

Western civilization grew out of two cultural branches – the Judeo-Christian and the Latin – which, if we really consider them deeply, are not that different in terms of their "hidden" roots. Is it possible to scientifically validate much of the way in which these traditions have empirically supposed the world can be understood? Is there any truth in these philosophical concepts? If so, how can we do that? Using mere metaphors!? We believe that both the so-called exact sciences and the human sciences are able to help us organize and order our thoughts. We know that thought doesn't arise *a priori*, but results from an act and from curiosity about natural phenomenon – a curiosity that drives us to find a way to explain them. A combination of mere theoretical speculation from the past and established scientific knowledge can reveal a culture that is sensitive and creative, or even "intuitive" if it comes close to some of the concepts accepted by modern science. An unprejudiced reading of authors as different as Plato and António Damásio, among others, allows us to discover theses that help us understand that which unites us and distinguishes us as humanity. On one thing, we can all agree – we have always been very curious and very creative. If we take these assumptions as our starting point, our abstract begins to make sense. What we want to show is that there is an interaction between the areas of knowledge of humanities and the exact sciences. In this article we will try to discover if there is a meeting point between these two branches of science, because I do believe there is.

1. Introduction

Curiosity undoubtly arises from quarreling. However, this kind of approach has been studied from several perspectives concerning the different scenarios based on exact sciences. In spite of their being exact sciences, we are also surprised by certain new possibilities, provided they are not absolute.

For example, some materials considered good electricity conductors were analysed by nanotechnologies as being exactly the opposite of what was initially considered. A similar situation happened with the Higgs particle (**Fig. 1**) which was once considered as 'God's particle'[Lederman & Teresi, 1993].

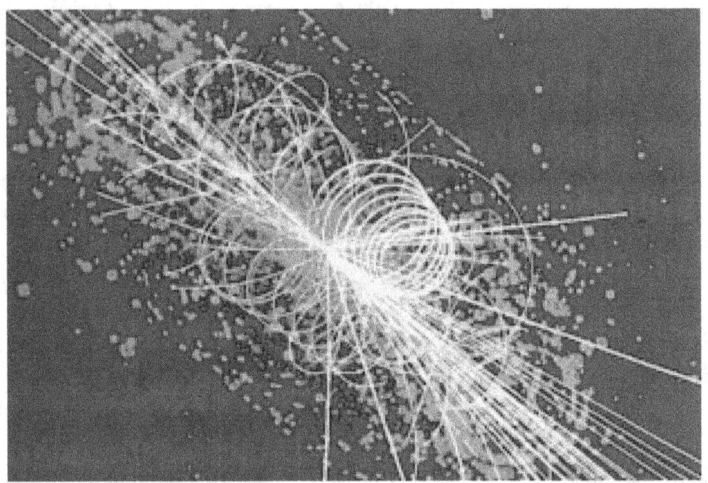

Fig. 1 – Simulation of a particle collision in which a Higgs boson is produced.

Scientific progress is achieved gradually and its validity is real; nevertheless, we need to find a meeting point for scientists and non-scientists to understand each other, so that they can proceed to a higher level of knowledge. Why do we need curiosity? Let us see:

— First of all, questions arise which define certain topics.
— Then, we can share our perplexity with others
— Finally, we can proceed to a deeper analysis.

2. Empirical Knowledge and Facts

Humanity has inherited several historic textbooks and related manuscripts that lead us to our actual stage of knowledge. This kind of methodology is characterized by our Greek tradition. Our ancestors have used empirical knowledge to explain some basic facts we observed in our daily life so we could better understand our world as well as better understand human beings. This kind of approach is still valid today while using curiosity, question and explanation. However, empiricism was not enough: to make laws we need a broader pool of data as well as deeper explanations so we can proceed to a generalization. In order to question whatever we want, we must use a working formula, such as:

— The subject (the one who observes)
— The object (the fact/phenomenon under study)
— Explanation (a given theory that supports the observed facts)

This methodology can be applied to everything in Nature in order to obtain a general culture whatever this culture may be. So, the question is: how to question knowledge or how did curiosity evolved since its very beginning, allowing human beings to perform such experiments? As a consequence, humanity has acquired more capacity to solve its own problems. Therefore, do we need to have different branches of knowledge, enhancing some of them? Perhaps not. How can we solve this cultural problem? When we have a paradoxical result is it completely wrong or may we have a small percentage of "true"? what we mean by this is the following:

The Schrödinger cat experiment raised a simple question: is the cat dead or alive?

If we analyze deeply some other experiments, similar situations can happen.

Now, another question I would like to ask: is Knowledge only worthwhile when there is an economic potential? Because, if that is the case, then Arts, as a form of knowledge, would not be necessary, since most of their works are considered by the great majority as having no economic potential at all. However, the arts market is flourishing. In the UK, for example, the Royal ballet is a major export. Similarly, publishers can become very rich by selecting best-selling novels and the market for buying and selling paintings has never been so good. Arts exhibitions can raise a lot of money. Surely, Art is a very successful branch of the economy, which employs a lot of people. It is highly competitive, so there are many artists who never become rich, but the economic potential is there.

However, let us consider in first place, the human being trying to understand how skills have evolved. According to António Damásio, a remarkable researcher in the neurosciences field, we know that, human knowledge started with feelings (**Fig. 2**).

Fig. 2 – The Feeling of What Happens: Body and Emotion in the Making of Consciousness

How did he reach this conclusion? First, the brain is considered as a biochemical organ with its chemical and biochemical substances, providing a way to act in a certain order so we can obtain a certain picture as if we had a film presentation. For Damásio, the perception of a given moment, should be experienced as a whole: it is like an integration of several images as part of a film production being made at the same time as we are choosing the soundtrack for that film. Now, this final picture takes place at the "mind". Antonio Damasio's new theory of the nature of consciousness and the construction of the self is the starting point for what Damásio calls the "The Feeling of What Happens" published in the year 1999.

Therefore, from 1999 on we are ready to feel what those actions produced in our brain picture and for this reason, the human being realizes that existence in himself is really true.

Now, how is the mind formed? This question is answered by Damásio:

— *"first we have the sensitive impressions in the brain known as "input" or trigger for a final result then perceived by the mind".*

For Damásio the main structure for mind formation is an association among images perception. So we can conclude that perception has got a key role in mind formation.

Let us have a look at the whole of Damásio's argument:

1. He explores the reasons that consciousness feels, well, conscious;
2. And he also integrates all this with emotions and feelings, making them play a central role in the experience of consciousness. He doesn't confine himself to the emotions that an observer could detect but addresses the feelings that only exist internally.
3. The nonconscious neural signaling of an individual organism begets the proto-self which permits core self and core

consciousness, which allow for an autobiographical self, which permits extended consciousness. At the end of the chain, extended consciousness permits conscience.

4. Consciousness is more than being awake, as one of Damasio's epileptic patients, suffering an absence-of-consciousness seizure, illustrates: ''Were you to have interrupted the patient at any point during the episode, he would not have known who you were; He would not know who he was or what he was doing.'' He might take a drink or open a door, but ''there would have been no plan, no forethought, no sense of wishing, wanting, considering, believing''.

5. Damasio's succinct summary of the mental process that consciousness entails: ''He would not have developed an image of knowing centered on a self; an enhanced image of the objects he was interacting with; a sense of the appropriate connection to what went on before each given instant or what might happen in the instant ahead''.

6. "You exist as a mental being when primordial stories are being told, and only then. You are the music while the music lasts."– this sentence illustrates quite well the whole Damásio's argument.

7. "The drama of the human condition comes solely from consciousness," Damasio says, and that allows us to create a better life, even though the price is high – not just the price of risk and danger and pain. It is the price of knowing risk, danger and pain; the price of knowing what pleasure is and knowing when it is missing or unattainable.

However, questions such as:

— What is the mind? how was it formed? When did it start? How did the brain develop? Have not yet been answered and there is considerable mystery around such thematics.

We must recognize our great ignorance within these fields of knowledge: Mind/Conscience/Brain. Therefore, we can only elaborate speculations about such topics, which even if they are wrong will be helpful for further studies.

Without these characteristics (perceptions, sensations, mind formation) the human being would not have the possibility to developed up to our cultural inheritance. A final result of what had been said we have:

— First we have a Sensation
— Second we have an Image   SENSATION – IMAGE – QUESTION
— Third we have a Question

3. Subject/Curiosity – Questioning/Explanation

Curiously, the sensation of being is part of a philosophical content, involving questions such as: who am I? Where did I come from? What is our final purpose? These questions are still not answered in spite of humanity's hard work to do so.

According to Damásio when he explains neurosciences he directs our attention to philosophy giving medical problems a philosophical dimension. Therefore, the "being" can be considered as a process instead of a "thing" and in this context we are simultaneously observers of others and ourselves; in this balance we are not only the process but also what is being processed.

Self-awareness raises the traditional philosophical question: the combination of body (as a biochemical entity) and consciousness (mind), allowing the formation of the conscious mind as part of our physical experience, resulting a final picture involving the "primordial feelings", a kind of image generated by the symbiosis body and brain interaction. This "primordial feelings" can only be achieved because there are certain properties of neurons, which are not yet recognized. For this reason this subject is still an open question to be studied within the neuroscience field.

The evolution of mankind, physically speaking is possible when taking all these aspects into consideration. For example, when we look at vocal cords we discover a new way to develop language as a communication agent of emotions and impressions.

These insights by Damásio offer us a better understanding of mind process building via the following scheme: **Sensation – Imageing – Questioning**

4. The several fields of Knowledge

The University is a strategy to unify multiple knowledge. In spite of the existence of Universities, all these different fields of knowledge, which were once considered as one body of content are now being analysed and reconstructed in a new light: the interdisciplinary approach where all fields meet others somehow.

The initial purpose of knowledge as a device to achieve a better comprehension of the world and ourselves has been replaced by economic interests above all: the supremacy of the material world over the cultural world. In this sense, if we consider an unstable economic society, this phenomena increases the danger of a bad manipulation of science for the worst purposes, such as an insufficient preservation of nature which we are part of as well as the lack of preservation of artistic values.

Through his friendship with Yo-Yo Ma, a well-known musician in the world of the violoncello, Damásio recognizes the complexity of physical and sensorial experiences that reveal the integrity of the musical work of art.

Sometimes, we witness the creation of artistic works which has nothing to do with mathematical logic in spite of our desire to achieve some kind of logic in those works. This means we are facing a structure common to scientists/ artists/philosophers: the consciousness of a mind that creates physical and abstracts images. The same can be said for poetry: there is no formula to explain it!

5. Humanism and the respect for the difference

Humanism is based upon values such as the respect for difference and on the principles that bring us together as a species amongst others.

According to Martin Heidegger, (1889-1976) in his seminal work *"Die Frage nach dem Ding"* when we reflect upon the "thing in itself" we can follow two pathways: we can visualize "the thing in itself" as an object or as an observer both being physical or not. Let us give an example, such as anxiety to make it clear. When we feel anxious we cannot necessary identify a material presence; however, every state of anxiety emerges from a cascade of biochemical substances that produces that stage which can be perfectly studied indirectly, of course.

Therefore, in each specific branch of knowledge we have a proper methodology to follow, which can and should be enhanced according to the latest achievements.

Considering the human being as a biopsychosociological entity according to Edgar Morin (1921 -) we can consider the human being as an entity to be studied within three different scientific fields:

a)   The biochemical
b)   The psychological
c)   The sociological

From this approach we have discovered a new direction given by Damásio in his works concerning brain studies in a deeper analysis in his latest book **(Fig. 3)** published in 2017. The author explains why feelings are an unstoppable force.

Fig. 3 – "The Strange Order of Things – Life, Feeling and the Making of Cultures

"What the body feels is every bit as significant as what the mind thinks" – Damásio argues in his latest book, turning to emotions to explain human consciousness and cultures.

6. The Order of Mind Formation

Descartes' Error: Emotion, Reason, and the Human Brain is a 1994 book **(Fig. 4)** written by neurologist António Damásio, in part a treatment of the mind/body dualism question. Damásio presents the "somatic marker hypothesis", a proposed mechanism by which emotions guide (or bias) behavior and decision-making, and positing that **rationality requires emotional input**.

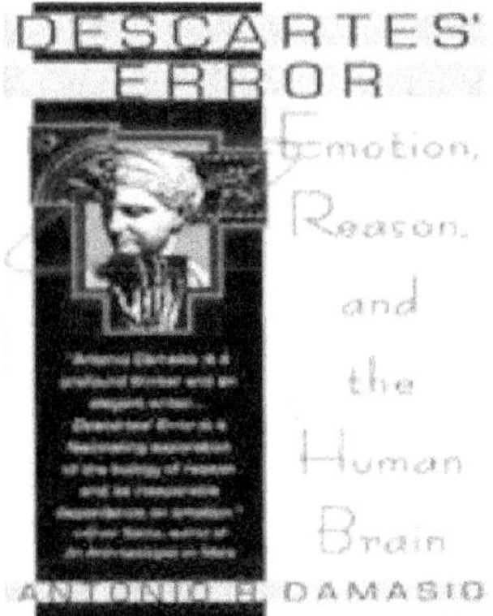

Fig. 4 – Descartes' Error

He argues that René Descartes' "error" was the dualist separation of mind and body, rationality and emotion. Therefore, Damásio argues that rationality stems from emotion, and that emotion stems from bodily senses; he refers to existence as being triggered by emotion and afterwards by rationality. *"Cogito, ergo sum"* (I think, therefore I am) was coined by the French philosopher René Descartes in his *Discourse on Method* (1637) as a first step in demonstrating the attainability of certain knowledge. However, later on in 2000 in his book "The Feeling of What Happens" Damásio recognizes that "Feeling is the first step for existence" not rationality, exactly in the same way as Baruch Espinosa (1632-1677) argued in the XVIIth century with the notion "I feel, therefore I am" in his writings.

The question raised by the dichotomy knowledge vs. questioning can be analysed through several approaches such as, Plato & Aristotle (384-322 B.C.) from the IV century B.C, Voltaire (1694-1788), Stephon Alexander (1971-...) and Richard Taylor, a trained painter and photographer, who adopted an interdisciplinary approach while studying natural patterns called fractals. He studied fractals in physics, psychology, physiology, geography, architecture and art.

Plato was the first to raise the knowledge question as we can see in his work "Menno", where he tried to prove that knowledge was inherited by birth. As Socrates disciple, he argued that ... *"Virtue as well as reminiscence are both directly dependent on our ancestral memories"*; so, the word "memory" can be seen as a keyword for knowledge acquisition.

While for Plato knowledge belonged to the world of Gods or the archetypal world, for us it has become a historical legacy.

Thinking or questioning a monologue or dialogue can be seen in every knowledge process either empirical or scientific in nature.

As an example of what has been said we have a Soren Kierkgaard (1813-1855) citation:

> ... *"Looking back we can understand life; in the same way, only by looking forward can we live our lives!"*

From Plato to Aristotle there is a great challenge by replacing the "essence of Gods" by the "essence of things" as being touchable. For example:

— Every tree is made up of roots, trunk and leaves and that is the tree essence as a whole. However, all trees are different from one another while keeping its identity: this is diversity in unity!

— Aristotle acts as the pioneer of the several branches of knowledge the same way as defended by Enlightenment in where the various Academies have emerged. Only in the XXth century have we witnessed the complete division of fields of knowledge into their different disciplines.

François-Marie Arouet, best known as Voltaire introduced the importance of Ethics as a fundamental concept with his work "The

Treatise On Intolerance" first published in 1763 where he is ridiculing intolerance; this book can also be considered in a broader perspective enclosing other sociological features, where the main characteristics of his position involve:

— Exclusion
— Dogmas
— Classification in a sense of a Division

Stephon Alexander in his work "The Jazz of Physics – The Secret Link between Music and the Structure of the Universe" (**Fig. 5**) published in 2016 show us how we can use analogies to bridge divisions between empirical knowledge and its scientific explanation.

Fig. 5 – The Jazz of Physics

The main question raised in this book is the following: "If the Universe's structure results from a vibration pattern, then what the hell causes such a vibration?" Being a jazz music and a physics professor he started to speculate how these two fields of knowledge could interact and the result was achieved in the so-called **musical mandala** (**Fig. 6**) elaborated by John Coltrane (1926-1967). In his research, he eventually found an analogy, in the music between musical notes and their relation to the celestial spheres.

This came from Greek Philosophy – of the Pythagorean School.

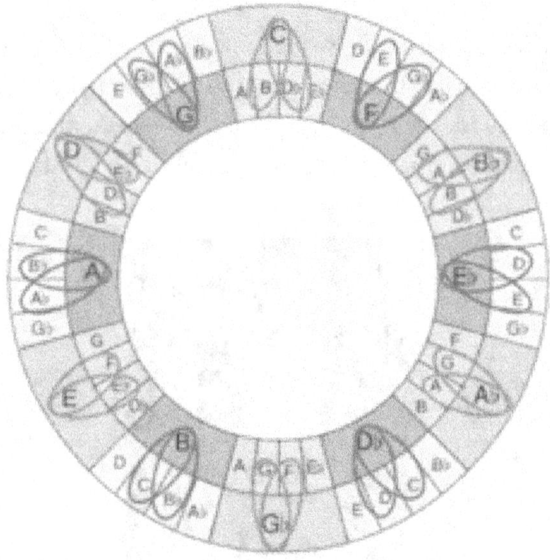

Fig. 6 – John Coltrane's musical mandala, in The Jazz of physics: the secret link between music and the structure of the universe

Richard Taylor looked for a universal natural order through the work of Jack Pollock (1912-1956). How did he do that? For Richard Taylor the work of Pollock can be understood as fractal modules representing the whole universe, which means that he was able to see through his eyes of a physicist giving his own explanation (**Fig. 7**).

Fig. 7 – Richard Taylor with a painting by Pollock, in Fractal Analysis of Pollock's Drip Paintings

However, the same situation can happen through the eyes of a chemist or mathematician or an artist or some other perspective. This results in a final goal: the unified perspective!

7. Conclusions

Throughout our reflection, we can establish an explanation of a certain phenomenon via opposite concepts, such as the atom concept. For example, Democritus proposed the indivisibility of atoms as a *hypothesis*, and his proposal was adopted many centuries later by chemists, which with the help of modern science established the divisibility of the same atom until quarks and further on. Depending on the devices we have the deeper we can go with our studies, enhancing a better understanding of the world around us. Let us raise a few questions which can be helpful for further research…Here we have a list of examples:

1 – Can we consider questioning a kind of knowledge, or just a pathway to achieve knowledge?

2 – Can we say that belief is knowledge?

3 – How many kinds of knowledge do we have?

4 – Can I be aware of something I don't know?

5 – Can I know something I am not aware of?

6 – Is knowledge wisdom?

7 – Can there be knowledge without awareness?

8 – Is knowledge without ethics advisable for a better world? (this question was already raised by the French author and Professor of Medicine Rabelais in the Renaissance in his often quoted remark: *Science sans conscience n'est que ruine de l'âme* (Science without conscience can but ruin the soul)

9 – What is perfection?

It is truly possible that the human being is a small piece of a greater universe, a vibration within a harmonic structure. A structure with a matrix, a multiplying element that unifies everything. Taylor concluded that the geometry of these vibrations representing the human being was fractal and Taylor went on to produce a technical analysis with a computer program (dimensional interplay analysis), and the results were very suggestive. Anyway, this method was used by Taylor on several paintings to confirm they were painted by Pollock, leading to the discovery of new works by the painter.

In order to maintain some coherence, this is a text that presents the reader with more questions than answers. We underline some important notions, such as:

— The brain is the organ that produces the mind, through sensations and images.

— The search for knowledge is an act of continuous curiosity and questioning, a characteristic common to all human beings.

— We should employ tolerance as a way to avoid dogma and prejudiced labels that inhibit freedom of thought, without which there is no creativity.

8. References

LEDERMAN, Leon & Dick TERESI (1993) **The God Particle**, 1993(ISBN 0-385-31211-3) and 2006 (ISBN 0-61871-168-6)

ALEXANDER, Stephon (2016) **The Jazz of physics: the secret link between music and the structure of the universe**, Perseus Books Group, Philadelphia, ISBN 9780465034994.

ARISTOTLE, (2000) **The Complete Works of Aristotle**, Cambridge University Press UK, ISBN 0 521 64017 2.

DAMÁSIO, António, (1999) **The Feeling of What Happens: Body and Emotion in the Making of Consciousness**, Mariner Books, ISBN 9780156010757.

DAMÁSIO, António, (1994) **Descartes Error**, Penguin Putnam, NY, ISBN 0-399-13894-3.

DAMÁSIO, António, (2003) **Looking for Spinoza: Joy, sorrow and the feeling brain**, Houghton Mifflin Harcourt Publishing Company, NY, 2003, ISBN 0-15-602871-9.

KLEIN, Jacob,(1965) **A Commentary on Plato Menno**, Unc Press Enduring Editions, ISBN 978-0-8078-7398-4

TAYLOR, Richard P. (1999) **Fractal Analysis of Pollock's Drip Paintings**, A.P. Micolich and D. Jonas in Nature, vol. 399, page 422, June 3.

VOLTAIRE, **Treatise on Intolerance**, Cambridge University Press, UK, 2000, ISBN 0 521 64017.

A look at the (my) creative process

Leonor Beltrán

This original idea for this text arose at the 2017 *Science Matters Conference*, when someone who had seen my individual exhibition at the Cascais Cultural Centre challenged me to write about my visual artistic work.

1. Introduction

To talk about my visual and performing art is to talk about myself, about the different and varied inner and creative experiences which I have known in my life and which structure and define me both as a person, and as a creator and artist in fields like Dance, Music and Drama. It is to talk about the paths I have travelled and the world that surrounds us and of which we are an integral part, in as much as nothing we are or achieve is independent of all the rest. Whether or not we are aware of this close relationship and union between ourselves, others and everything that exists doesn't alter the fact or its reality. Union or disunion with others and everything is one of the things that highlight some of the differences between human beings and their consciousnesses. The way we live, which ought to include having the courage, or not feeling afraid, to look deep within ourselves, not only requires a state of understanding and awareness of the sphere in which our person is an entity that is fully-fledged in terms of its different components (to my mind, above all the spiritual element), but also a constant attentiveness to the way in which we relate and cohabit with others and with everything that exists, visible and invisible, making all these processes part of that which defines us and can bring us close to a true identity and a possibility of becoming the Being we are. The border between us, others and everything is very narrow, and it is with this consciousness, which requires an introspection or a capacity for self-awareness, and an empathic closeness to the other and the world, without fears and in consonance with the different forces that inhabit and surround us, that the creative process takes place.

2. The one who creates

The one who creates is simultaneously a channel, a receiver, a moderator and a creator – i.e. someone who is capable of listening, feeling, thinking, having ideas, transmuting different universes into immanent or non-material materialisations. To me, the essence of the act of creation itself results from an experience of spiritual immanence, an inner state of attentiveness, which can gain access to dimensions of another nature that connect us to everything and are part of us, and in which all the inner forces and realities, including our deepest self – the soul – are invited to take part in a dialogue. And it is out of the nature of this inner dialogue between us, everything and the work itself that the latter's nature and the substance which defines it are born. Creative processes are multiple and their sources are extremely varied, and when they take shape, they acquire a soul, presence and meaning thanks to their creator's nature and essence. That essence is reflected and is both passed on and assimilated by the work, inasmuch as because it is someone's creation, that work is itself an extension of that someone, an emanation, a reflection of that being, their nature, personality, consciousnesses, intelligences, culture, education and experiences and the different inner forces and energies which cohabit in, manage, dominate and define them. A work's soul emanates from its creator and is a reflection of their content, inner state and consciousness. So the work's strength and quality come not just from the technical, aesthetic and artistic aspects, but beyond that, from the life breathed into it by the creator, who infuses a variety of things into it including their essence, nature, temperament and capacity to capture and create.

3. The Origin of the Creative Process

Whatever the origin of the creative process, the origin of the ideas and the creator's conviction about and understanding of life and the world, a work of art always acquires an essence, a soul, a strength and a quality that is very much its own and unique. So whether one thinks or believes that the origin of artistic creation is of a spiritual order, transcendent, or simply pertains to the material world and all the different corporeal realities, be they to do with mental faculties, the senses, sensitivities, the feelings, the emotions or biochemical impulses, or derives from a close relationship and partnership between all these elements, which are not dissociated from one another but rather form part of the human whole, a work of art is always marked by an essence and quality of some kind. A work of art is in its own right a gift, an act of sharing the artist's own intimacy, which they give to the world. A work that has emanated from the one who made it and is revealed and projected to the other and the world in the act of its creation. A work of art is an extension of the artist that takes on an existence and content of its own, ceasing to belong to them at the moment at which it is exhibited, and thereby acquiring a status of independence from its creator and becoming part of the world and of humanity.

The creative process needs time and space, inner space, space close to the object that is being created and space away from it, from everything else that surrounds us and sometimes even from parts of ourselves and from interferences that can distract us from the process, inasmuch as the act of creation requires seclusion, total dedication, attention, respect and a full relationship with the work. The creative process is above all a space of attentiveness and an inner listening, and simultaneously an act of courage and freedom of action. The one who creates has to have the capacity to perform the action, to be able to do, to not hesitate, and to allow the creation to bloom without censuring it and without being afraid of its outcome. We have to let the work speak, breathe and take on life. Neither an awareness and understanding of the processes, nor their apparent absence, affect the act of creation in itself, or its existence, inasmuch as that act is one of constant discovery, creativity, imagination and mastery and simultaneously of submission and sublimation of the self to itself, the creative act and the work that is being born and created. The different consciousnesses or absences of understanding are no more than human states at moments in time, which tend to change and be altered by the process itself. To quote Isaac Newton, in the face of the creative process and a work of art, we often also seem like *only a child playing on the beach, while vast oceans of truth lie undiscovered before me.*[1] So when we look at the creative process and the universe of Art and we try to understand, define and control it, however creative, capable, intelligent, cultured and informed we may be, more often than not we seem like a child playing at the seaside while the vast universe of Art and creation stretch out before us. The infinite extends in front of us in the shape of a something that has yet to be discovered, and it is from

---

[1] Cited from http://thinkexist.com/quotes/isaac_newton/ on 28.04.2008: *To myself I am only a child playing on the beach, while vast oceans of truth lie undiscovered before me.*

this source, which surrounds us and of which we are a part, that the artist will drink and look for their inspiration, their truth, because that which is inside is outside and that which is outside is inside – we only have to be attentive, to learn to listen, see, understand, trust and feel.

4. The Creative Process and Multiple Universes

If we associate the creative process with a dimension of multiple universes and spaces that possess "infinite" frontiers, which surround us, englobe us and inhabit us to the degree or level of our awareness of them and in which different aspects and strengths (such as our soul, our nature and our individual component parts, others and the world) exist and cohabit, the multiple questions related with the creative process and the Work of Art may perhaps take on much vaster outlines than just that of a concentric, egocentric and materialist way of looking at things which depends solely on the domain of individual liberties, technical abilities and the individual's wills, desires, creativities, intelligences and understandings. So questions like: where does the creative process arise from, where are ideas, imagination, the capacity to create, the originality of a work and its soul, essence and nature or their absence generated and where do they come from, and thus what gives a work the status of a Work of Art, are questions which, although they can't be understood and explained in just one way, may perhaps begin to be answered by looking at them in a manner that englobes this possibility of different inner and outer dimensions and different degrees of consciousness, sources and procedural supports. In reality, a work of art is the result of the nature, information, culture, capacities and universes to which the creating artist has access, and therefore also of the whole of, or the spark of, a vision which they grasp, process and finally transform.

Human beings have always sought to find an explanation, a definition of what Art might be, and if they can't find one, they categorise it as something that can't be consensually defined. That definition is increasingly part of a rhetorical limbo whose intelligible complexity grows in proportion to the ever-increasing diversity of the artistic universe and its works, the ever-vaster complexity of knowledge and the variety of human cultures, interests, intelligences and understandings involved.

5. The contemporary art world

The contemporary art world, which is both more and more fragmented and more and more averse to the commitment of definition, in that it is confronted with the miracle of the multiple and the diverse that tends to break with safe, identifiable processes, is ironically tending to create control mechanisms by all kinds of means and for all kinds of reasons – the need for power or self-affirmation, fears, desires to dominate, interests, ignorance, lack of understanding, tastes/ appreciations, empathies, different perceptions, fashions or lobbies… A work that is born out of an inner truth, a free and attentive nature, a creative and artistic need combined with a capacity to think, feel and understand the other and the world without fears and taboos, scares normality. True Art and a true creative process do not entail boundaries, restrictions, impositions; they aren't linear or subject to the same, single set of rules and they can't be domesticated and controlled. All the educations, techniques, tools, methodologies, Schools, fashions, aesthetic senses and concepts are no more than supports – doubtless very important or even fundamental to an individual's training, but nonetheless not capable of explaining and bringing about the birth of a creator and a Work of Art. Human capacity to create art transports us to the domain of the sublime, to faculties that combine within themselves subtle states of perception from which the gift and the genius are summoned. The act of artistic creation calls on a heightened dimension of inner availability and attentiveness, without boundaries or fears of going deep into oneself, others and the world. Everything interacts, independently of our own consciousness, and art is the expression of those multiple realities.

6. What is Art?

Art is communication, expression, imagination, transformation, innovation, contamination, urgency, intuition, an extension of..., an accumulation of..., a meeting or a failure to come together, a confrontation. Well, at the end of the day, art is above all an act of creation on a human scale and a mirror of that same humanity. Art is a path for searchers, one that gives birth to something that doesn't exist yet or is hidden. Art reflects diversity, the whole, time and the consciousnesses and states of being of beings, nature and things. Art can reveal and create new realities, transmute, reformulate, uncover, illuminate, put into (new) perspective, resize, cover up and hide, and as such, demands new ways of seeing and feeling, new approaches and readings of the world, life, human beings and everything that exists. Art takes courage, strength and a strong creative experience. Art requires the absence of the fear of exposing oneself, of being and allowing to be. Art has as much the capacity to destroy, undo, crumple and corrupt as it does to build, awaken, transform, innovate, protest, question, invoke new realities and elevate Human Beings and make them more alive and aware, because Art is energy, movement and a reflection of human culture seen as an expression and living manifestation of human essence and nature. Art is life, matter and spirit; at its most profound, in my view, Art is a miracle of the divine that exists and manifests in us through that which we are. I see this "miracle of the divine" as part of a dimension that is inherent in human beings, a possibility that underlies our inner self, a connection, a channel which we can open or not and which links us to the Whole and to everything. Art is a path that makes it easier to pass from the invisible to the visible and vice versa. Art is the expression of the Being, its parts and its whole, and thus also of its soul and its spiritual element, which is an integral part of that whole. The diversity of art and the multiplicity of artistic works are the fruit of the different aspects that characterise human nature and a reflection of human cultures, sensibilities, thoughts and consciousnesses, both individual and collective. Art mirrors humanity and the wholeness which exists in each one of us and which reveals itself in everything, via both everything and ourselves. In its primordial essence, the creative process entails an individual act made either by a person, a being, a unique nature, or by the conjugation of several people, beings and natures, and one whose result tends to generate a work, which is itself also unique and unrepeatable.

According to Heidegger: *What art is we should be able to gather from the work. What the work is we can only find out from the nature of art.*[2] However, irrespective of the philosophical question underlying the essence of art, the object that is the work in itself, and where it comes from, the reality is that the one who renders it possible, makes, sees, hears and/or feels it and attributes value to it in this world (in principle!), is the human being themselves. Regardless of whether or not art possesses an existence of its own, in its own right it belongs

---

[2] Martin Heidegger, "The Origin of the Work of Art" (German: *Der Ursprung des Kunstwerkes*), in Martin Heidegger, *Off the Beaten Track,* ed./trans. Young, Julian and K. Haynes, Cambridge University Press, 2001, p.2.

to and is a manifestation of human nature, either through the process of creation, perception, appreciation, conservation or codification, or as a result of the pure discovery that can happen by means of the sensitive act of observation and enjoyment. As such, and once again in Heidegger's words:

> *The artist is the origin of the work. The work is the origin of the artist. Neither is without the other. Nevertheless, neither is the sole support of the other. Artist and work* are *each, in themselves and in their reciprocal relation, on account of a third thing, which is prior to both; on account, that is, of that from which both artist and artwork take their names, on account of art.*
>
> *As the artist is the origin of the work in a necessarily different way from the way the work is the origin of the artist, so it is in yet another way, quite certainly, that art is the origin of both artist and work.*[3]

7. Art, Work and Artist

Art, Work and Artist are in themselves one *corpus*, interconnected by the fusion between the creator, the artistic and creative process and the work itself. But it is via the creator/artist's capacity to give rise to something they feel and that exists within or outside them, and to be connected to that something and express themselves through that which may be Art, that the content and essence of that which is created can become a Work of Art. So, regardless of the origin of Art and the Work, it is via the origin and existence of the human being, of the artist who creates, that Art and the Work acquire a presence as realities which are to be experienced in this world and this material

---

[3] Ibid., p.1.

and existential dimension. Art and Work are born or reborn, taking on life through the artist's capacity to create and transmute, perceive or connect with them and their sources. But artist and human being are one and the same, so the identity of the being that creates and their capacity to seize, think, structure and do something that underlies an immaterial reality are dynamic, due to the relationship between creator and work. The work reflects its creator. At the same time, the one who identifies the work and attributes it the value of a Work of Art in this world is a human being, be they artist or not, and it is in the two-way relationship between creator and source and in the way in which the creative process unfurls and the work is materialised that lies the question of a Work of Art. Creator and source become one, and both give rise to the work of art. The source inspires the artist, who in turn takes it as theirs and lends it visibility, while the source becomes an integral part of the artist and the two become one. The artist simultaneously becomes source, origin and vessel, and the work becomes art through the artist's artistic and creative content.

In essence, the creation of an artistic work or a work of art is the result of an autonomous process between the creator and the work, which takes place as part of the intimate relationship with what, let's say, are "their" forces and energies. I use the terms "forces" and "energies" because they serve to identify my feeling and the invisible reality which I see as going beyond an exclusively material and biochemical approach to life, thereby enabling me to put a name to a whole range of subtle nuances that live within us and manage and identify us as human beings. These forces and energies not only exist within us but are an integral part of life and of everything that exists, providing us with distinct spaces of imagination and creativity which, in turn, through the creator/artist's nature and capacity to perceive and relate with the forces and energies, give rise to, and imprint and determine the identity, content and soul of, the work that is created. Just like life, a work of art is born out of a dynamic process, a flow of energies, transmutations and cohabitations between and of everything that consciously and unconsciously exists within the creator. The creative act in itself begins with a process of inner dialogues which, while it is invisible, is generated by the creator's experience and capacity to structure and materialise different consciousnesses, ideas, images, thoughts and feelings in visible and/or invisible and permanent, momentary and/or ephemeral ways. The creative act comes from a moment when something is grasped and then materialised.

A Work of Art is generated by the one who lives, creates and lends body and life to an "idea" and makes something that didn't previously exist be born, and not by one who limits themselves to copying or plagiarising. The latter engages in a process that is empty of identity, in that they take on the identity of another, a third party, tending to produce works that are neutral and sometimes even entirely devoid of life and content, in that they lack substance because there is no inner experience; unlike the former, whose living inner experience means they are the creator of a Living Work, the product of a real process, of a constant dialogue and discovery that arises between creator and work. A true creation is derived from an identity with a content that gives the work its essence. A work that has content touches, communicates with and penetrates the other in the most varied ways, awakening a huge diversity of feelings, thoughts and ways of seeing. The human diversity of perspectives and feelings gives rise to different forms of looking and understanding in the way in which works of art are perceived, felt, understood and accepted.

The characteristics and capacities that each individual develops over the course of their life are primarily the result of themselves, their environment, others, education, and generations that preceded them. Their evolution is derived not only from the experiences and the decisions they have taken during their lifetime, but also from their inner dimension, which in my view is intimately linked to their "Spiritual" dimension. The latter entails an inner process that happens both within and outside time, within a framework that can't be measured, weighed or seen, but can be identified through the individual's actions, life paths, achievements and created works. What defines our human content, our identity, our nature and essence? Everything. Everything we are and we go through is mirrored within us and spreads throughout us at every inner and outer level, in what we are, in the way in which we relate with and see the world, in the balance or imbalance of our personality and character, our consciousness, intelligence, judgement and wisdom, and thus in the degree of our humanity. A work of art mirrors a part, parts, or all of this.

8. Talking about my work

To talk about my work is to look closely at the multiple inner movements and energies that arise and live within me, in an intimate relationship and cohabitation with everything. It is to talk about my awareness of myself, of others and of everything that exists. It is especially to talk about the importance of the Dance and Music that have always accompanied me in my life. To me, both of them – dance and music – are the living expression of life and its movement. To talk about my work is to talk about all the deep experiences that dance, music and drama have given me, and about what they have added to my overall development and the process of gaining new and more encompassing understandings and awarenesses of life, my being, others, the word and all the various visible and invisible universes. It is to talk about a whole creative, imaginative, perceptive and sensitive universe that dance, music and drama have developed in me. It is to talk about the senses that have acquired new dimensions and have sharpened the total awareness of the body, other bodies and their energies, of a whole awakening that has made me more alert and attentive to visible and invisible, organic, audible, spatial, aesthetic, relational, creative and sublime realities. But it is above all to also talk about my spiritual path and the place it occupies in my life. I am talking about spirituality in the sense of a constant energetic feeling, something natural, an active and expansive inner experience and consciousness, a life force which pulsates, is vibrant and which, just like the act of breathing, feeds, builds and inhabits me and by its essence defines me as a Human Being; not in the sense of a spirituality seen as transcendent, something that comes to us from elsewhere, that exists somewhere outside, that passes through us and doesn't belong to us. To me, the spiritual is a permanent source of energy that cohabits in a continuous symbiosis with the whole of my being, of what I am and what I do. I am talking about a spiritual that nurtures life itself and is an integral part of everything and thus of both me and others. I am talking about a reality that can make us more complete and more human. I am talking about an consciousness that comes from our soul and feeds and guides us.

So to talk about my visual artistic work is to talk about the different states of consciousness that are nothing more than subtle dialogues between forces which confront one another and metamorphose in a constant game of affirmation, staking a place, giving way and living together, all of which manifests itself primarily through feelings, emotions and thoughts, and about an entire vibrant energetic universe that pullulates inside and outside me, speaks to me and manifests in different layers and consciousnesses. It is to talk about sensations that become perceptions, ideas and thoughts that in turn become creations. It is to talk about another consciousness which can show me dimensions that lie beyond my own body and its movement, and which manifests itself through my actions, expressions, ideas and different creative acts. It is to talk about the constant symbiosis between my inner and my outer, between I, others, us and everything that exists, both visible and invisible. It is to talk about the various ways of looking that have conjugated and agglomerated within me over time and with my life experience and can express themselves in countless ways, through a movement, a gesture, a sound, a rhythm, a silence, a word, a thought, an emotion, a feeling, a brush or pen-stroke which propagates itself ephemerally and which the paper absorbs and materialises, capturing for itself that which is eternal and invisible to the eyes, an image which allows itself to be imprisoned and which captivates, captivates us and raises us up, involves us and welcomes us in, in its sensitive tangibility.

In the case of the visual arts, the inner movements that I feel express themselves through the materialisation of a gesture that becomes a brush or pen-stroke, and each stroke expresses one or more ways of seeing these inner movements. By giving shape and meaning to an interiority, to a feeling that inhabits and defines me, my work seeks to lend shape, space and time to the corporality and incorporality that constantly accompany me. So I could say that I am looking to follow and manifest the different movements that live within me, from the macro to the micro, from the micro to the macro. Expressing them tends to create both different and repetitive structures, in an interlinked web of forms that dance on the paper, recreating rhythmic, audible, scenic and choreographic inner landscapes. My china-ink drawings take on different textures and shades, depending on the density of the ink and the pictorial relationship between lines, dots, forms and blots, some of which are made with a pen and some with a brush. In them I discover paths, labyrinths, nature, figures and a variety of abstract shapes that gradually reveal themselves to the gaze and come out of the paper, sometimes creating an illusion of three dimensionality and/ or vibrant movements that agitatedly move on the paper. In my work

I seek to imprint breath, life and dynamic onto the drawing or the painting; I seek to lend shape, voice and corporality to my inner, my being and everything that traverses and lives within it, in a permanent relationship with the personal, collective and universal whole. To me, to create is a need, a truly urgent need to communicate and express; it is the possibility of lending voice and form to my inner. To me, the act of creation is a manifestation of existence and a reflection of the life that pulses and lives within me, defines me and opens and connects me to others and everything that exists.

9. Conclusion

In conclusion, I would say that the origin of a work of art may lie in a series of "sources" inside and outside the human being, but in my view, in essence, it is the result of a life quest, the Being's quest to Be, its need to go beyond itself, its creative, inventive and "expressive" need as a manifestation of its living interiority, its corporeal, vital, energetic and spiritual identity. Art creates new ways of looking at existence, brings freedoms and provides a means of encountering and fully affirming a human being. Its language enables a human being to see, recreate or discover and generate new realities, other worlds and universes, providing pathways that allow the invisible, the hidden, the incommunicable to transmute, transform, reveal itself and take on an existence of its own through the artist's capacity to create, engender, materialise and give life to new ideas. Art reveals the invisible and makes it visible to us. To a greater or lesser extent, art opens up the possibility for human beings to connect to Everything and the Divine itself. This quest reflects our inner dimension and complexity, our humanity and our capacity to go beyond our limits and be able to achieve an understanding and a wider and much larger human and universal consciousness than usual. To paraphrase Bapak Muhammad Subuh Sumohadiwidjojo, culture is a supreme expression of freedom, because it enables us to develop in accordance with our own talents and thus with our own nature, rather than simply imitating others or doing what others want or expect of us.[4]

Art takes on existence, be it visible, invisible, permanent or ephemeral, and reveals the symbolic, imaginative and creative human universe. Works can acquire the status of something that is alive – of a Work of Art – with the ability to touch, transform and change the dimension of the other and the human universe itself. Art reveals the different layers of things and of the human beings who create them. Art calls on the Divine and the Human which exist in each of us and which, through their subtle and singular nature, appear shrouded in a profound mystery – the mystery of the Human Soul, Life and Creation.

---

[4] Bapak Muhammad Subuh Sumohadiwidjojo, "Universal Culture", in Loving your fellow man, Tunbridge Wells, Subud Publications International, 1984, p.34-35.

www.ingramcontent.com/pod-product-compliance
Lightning Source LLC
Chambersburg PA
CBHW070121260726
48658CB00001B/211